# Cases in Financial Accounting

## Accounting

### A PRINCIPLES-BASED APPROACH

# Cases in Financial Accounting

## A PRINCIPLES-BASED APPROACH

ALAN J. RICHARDSON, EDITOR
YORK UNIVERSITY

THOMSON

NELSON

Australia    Canada    Mexico    Singapore    Spain    United Kingdom    United States

**THOMSON**

**NELSON**

Cases in Financial Accounting: A Principles-Based Approach

by Alan J. Richardson, Editor

**Associate Vice President, Editorial Director:**
Evelyn Veitch

**Executive Editor:**
Rod Banister

**Senior Marketing Manager:**
Charmaine Sherlock

**Developmental Editor:**
Natalie Barrington

**Permissions Coordinator:**
Nicola Winstanley

**Copy Editor/Proofreader:**
Matthew Kudelka

**Production Coordinator:**
Cathy Deak

**Design Director:**
Ken Phipps

**Interior Design:**
Katherine Strain

**Cover Design:**
Sasha Moroz

**Compositor:**
Interactive Composition Corporation

**Printer:**
Transcontinental

**Library and Archives Canada Cataloguing in Publication**

Richardson, Alan J. (Alan John), 1955–
    Cases in financial accounting : a principles-based approach / Alan J. Richardson.

ISBN 0-17-610275-2

    1. Accounting—Case studies.
I. Title.

HF5635.R52 2006        657'.044
C2005-907507-4

# CONTENTS

# TABLE OF FIGURES

# PREFACE

This book owes much to the work of L.S. (Al) Rosen. Al Rosen saw the need for a principles-based approach to financial accounting that would allow users and preparers to see the substance beneath the form of business transactions and to cope with new transactions and changing circumstances in an appropriate way. It is an approach that requires the development and use of critical thinking skills and the application of a sound knowledge of what financial accounting is trying to accomplish in society. Al Rosen put his philosophy to work in his teaching style and in his publications. A generation of accountants benefited from his courses and still tells stories of being harangued, insulted, but, most of all, educated in the subtleties of financial accounting. Rosen retired from York University in 2000 but remains active in the forensic accounting firm that bears his name. Since the failure of Enron and the accounting scandals at other companies, Rosen's warnings and his approach to financial reporting have gained even greater credibility as an appropriate way to train those who will report to the capital markets, audit those reports, or rely on financial statements to make investment and other economic decisions.

## FEATURES OF THIS TEXT

This case book provides realistic snapshots of business practice. Many of the cases are based on situations that were covered in the financial press and represent decisions that were faced by managers, auditors, and investors, often with severe consequences. The cases represent a range of businesses including small, family-owned enterprises, medium-sized businesses, and large corporations. The range of situations covered provides a realistic reflection of the environment that will be faced by the graduates of top business and accounting programs.

This book features *short* multiple-issue, transaction-oriented cases. The cases are short enough—typically only a few pages—that they can be used as a supplement to traditional lecture-based courses. The cases are rich enough, however, that they could form the basis for a full case course. Regardless of the setting, the cases allow students to practise the skills they will be using in their future careers. Specifically, the cases require students to:

- identify relevant information in complex circumstances based on theoretical models and frameworks;
- apply analytical models to diagnose and understand causes and consequences;
- develop group skills, including an appreciation for alternative points of view;
- practise problem solving and generating realistic alternative courses of action;
- practise decision making and the application of criteria in making choices;
- justify recommendations based on evidence, logic, and authoritative guidance; *and*
- communicate analyses and conclusions to others.

The introductory material in the book includes a discussion of "principled judgment"—an approach to choosing among accounting alternatives that underlies recent pronouncements by securities regulators and accounting standard setters. Principled judgment represents a process of choice that is guided and constrained by the objectives of financial statements in society. We also include a guide to case analysis and two "solved" cases featuring footnotes that lead the student through the decisions that were made to construct the recommendations provided. We believe that the approach used in this book will help educate the thoughtful managers and accounting practitioners that are needed in today's society.

All of the cases have been tested in the classroom, as assignments, or in an examination setting. The teaching notes reflect the way the case writer originally used the case and may include key discussion points, possible alternative approaches to the issues in the case, and, in some cases, detailed grading keys for cases that were used on examinations. The teaching notes also provide suggestions for using the cases, including four recommended sets of cases from the book to cover introductory financial accounting at the undergraduate or MBA level.

## ACKNOWLEDGMENTS

The cases in this book have been tested on students in the Bachelor of Business Administration program (BBA) and Master of Business Administration (MBA) program at the Schulich School of Business, York University, Canada. These students have high aspirations and keen intellects; they have challenged their instructors to produce materials that encourage them to develop the skills they will need in business. We are grateful for the opportunity to refine these materials in their classrooms. We would also like to thank Rosamaria Tassone and Sachpreet Chandhoke, who read through an early draft and helped select the cases and arrange them into a book.

We would also like to thank reviewers who provided valuable feedback on the first draft. Thanks to Jocelyn King, University of Alberta; K. Nainar, McMaster University; Aziz Rajwani, Langara College; and Bob Sproule, University of Waterloo.

Finally, I thank Teresa Colavecchia, who provided administrative support for this project. Teresa was thanked by Al Rosen in his original case book; she continues to be the heart of the accounting area at the Schulich School of Business.

# CONTRIBUTING AUTHORS

**Kathryn Bewley** is an associate professor of accounting and auditing at York University with appointments in the Schulich School of Business and the Atkinson School of Administrative Studies. She holds a PhD from the University of Waterloo and is a chartered accountant. Her research examines the impact of financial reporting regulation and disclosure, the value and relevance of accounting information, audit quality, and corporate environmental reporting; it has been published in the *Journal of International Financial Management, Advances in Environmental Management and Accounting,* and *CA Magazine.* She teaches financial accounting, accounting theory, auditing, and information systems and is involved in the development of technology-enhanced teaching methods.

**Catherine Byers** is a contract instructor of accounting at the Schulich School of Business and Seneca College. She is a member of the ICAO and holds an MBA from Wilfrid Laurier University. Besides teaching, she provides business advisory services to clients in the real estate and retail sectors.

**Carl K.L. Ching,** a tax manager in the Industrial and Automotive Products Group with KPMG LLP in Toronto, is a part-time accounting instructor with the Schulich School of Business, where he received his BBA degree (with distinction). He is a chartered accountant, certified public accountant, and certified financial planner and has also completed Parts I and II of the In-depth Tax Course. In addition, he participates actively in the chartered accountant qualification process, provides counselling services on case-writing techniques, and was a marker of the CICA's Uniform Final Exam.

**Elizabeth J. Farrell** is an adjunct professor at the Schulich School of Business. In both 1999 and 2003 she was awarded the Seymour Schulich Award for Teaching Excellence; she was also nominated for the award in 2004 and 2005. She holds degrees from Queen's University (BA/BPHE) and York University (MBA). She has served at the ICAO as a seminar leader and as an assistant coordinator at the School of Accountancy. She is a member of the Education, Program, Administration and Examination Committee. She is the coauthor of *Advanced Financial Accounting* and author of an accounting case analysis software package, study guides, professional development courses, and other case materials.

**Arthur R. Guimaraes** is a lecturer in the accounting area at the Schulich School of Business. He is also a senior financial analyst in business planning at Manulife Financial. He holds a BBA from the Schulich School of Business (with distinction, 1999) and is a chartered accountant (2002) and a chartered business valuator (2004).

He has been nominated for the Seymour Schulich Award for Teaching Excellence (2003) and has taught at the ICAO's School of Accountancy (2005).

**Elizabeth M. LaRegina** is a PhD candidate in accounting at the Schulich School of Business. She is a chartered accountant (Ontario) and holds an MBA from Schulich. Before embarking on her PhD, she worked in the financial services industry for more than fifteen years in a variety of senior positions in accounting, auditing, and human resources. Her research interests include auditor behaviour, the subject of her dissertation. She was the recipient of the Canadian Academic Accounting Association's 2003 Case Competition Award.

**Prem M. Lobo** is an instructor and course coordinator in the accounting area of the Schulich School of Business and is an associate with Rosen & Associates, litigation and forensic accountants. He holds a BBA (with distinction) from the Schulich School of Business and is a chartered accountant, chartered business valuator, and certified public accountant. He is the editor of *Expert Insights*, a quarterly publication of LECG Canada, and has published in *Lawyer's Weekly*. He is a contributing editor to *Understanding Financial Analysis in Litigation* by Errol Soriano.

**Alan T. Mak** is a senior associate with Rosen & Associates Limited, litigation and forensic accountants. He holds a BBA (with distinction) from the Schulich School of Business and is a chartered accountant, chartered business valuator, and certified public accountant in Illinois and Hong Kong. He has provided expert opinion evidence before the Ontario Superior Court in the areas of financial accounting, income tax, economic damages, and forensic accounting. He has held teaching appointments at the Schulich School of Business and the University of Toronto.

**Kevin Markle** is an adjunct professor of financial accounting at the Schulich School of Business. He is a chartered accountant and certified financial planner and holds a BSc from the University of North Carolina at Chapel Hill and a BEd from the University of Toronto. He is a two-time winner of the Seymour Schulich Award for Teaching Excellence. He is a seminar leader at the ICAO's School of Accountancy and has marked noncomprehensive simulations of the CICA's Uniform Final Examination.

**Alan J. Richardson** is professor and chair of the accounting area at the Schulich School of Business. He holds a PhD from Queen's University and is an FCGA and Life Member of the Certified General Accountants Association of Ontario. He was the founding editor of *Canadian Accounting Perspectives* and currently sits on the editorial boards of ten academic journals. His research focuses on the development of accounting institutions, including standard-setting processes and the regulation of audit practice rights. He has published in *Accounting Organizations and Society, Contemporary*

*Accounting Research, Journal of Accounting Research,* and *Accounting Historians Journal,* among others.

**Anthony Scilipoti** is executive vice-president and a founding partner of the independent equity research firm, Veritas Investment Research Corporation. He is a chartered accountant and certified public accountant and serves on the CICA's Emerging Issues Committee. Over the past several years, he has published numerous research reports critical of the accounting at major firms such as Nortel, Celestica, Royal Group Technologies, Alliance Atlantis, CGI, Bombardier, and CAE. He is also a part-time accounting instructor in the MBA and BBA programs at the Schulich School of Business, where he was nominated for the Teaching Excellence award in both 1997 and 2003.

**Viswanath Umashanker Trivedi** is an assistant professor in the accounting area at the Schulich School of Business. He is a chartered accountant in India and holds a PhD from Arizona State University. His research, primarily using the methodology of experimental economics, focuses on ethical and behavioural issues in taxation, auditing, and financial accounting. He work has been published in the *Journal of Business Ethics, Behavioral Research in Accounting,* and the *Canadian Tax Journal.* He was involved in changing the accounting curriculum to the decision and users' focus at Arizona State University under a $1 million grant from the Accounting Education Change Commission.

**Dilsat Tuna** is a chartered accountant and a lecturer in the accounting area at the Schulich School of Business. She holds a BBA from the Schulich School of Business and is a member of the Institute of Chartered Accountants of Ontario. She is currently working as a Manager of Assurance and Advisory Services at Williams and Partners Chartered Accountants in Markham. In addition to working full time in public practice, she has devoted a significant portion of her time to accounting education and to providing training courses for students writing the Uniform Final Exam in order to become a chartered accountant.

# CHAPTER 1

# THE CASE FOR CASES

The decision by your professor to use cases to teach financial accounting has not been made lightly. When the objective of a course of study is to provide you with a body of knowledge, such as a set of facts to be memorized, then readings and lectures may be a more efficient form of learning. But being an effective user or preparer of financial accounting information is not simply a matter of knowing how to do the bookkeeping. Financial reporting is an attempt to capture the essence of complex business transactions in a concise manner and to communicate this essence to a variety of organizational stakeholders. In this process, management must make numerous choices about how to recognize, measure, and disclose the events that have occurred. These choices will affect the interests of many parties. This means that in accounting for business transactions there are legitimate alternatives that can be used to capture what happened. As a user, preparer, or auditor of financial accounting reports, you must be able to identify the alternatives that could have been used, as well as the consequences to users of financial statements of those different alternatives. Furthermore, you must be able to defend your preferences for reporting the transaction.

In order to understand and participate in the financial reporting process, you will need to develop certain skills, including the ability to analyze complex information, make critical judgments, and communicate your findings persuasively to others. These skills cannot be developed by rote memorization. We believe these skills can best be developed by using cases in the classroom. The types of skills and knowledge we would like you to take away from your studies require that you be actively involved in the learning process — that is the pedagogic case for cases. Furthermore, if you are considering a career as a professional accountant, or using accounting as a stepping stone to senior management or consulting positions, or working as a management consultant or financial analyst, you will be required to demonstrate the skills that case analysis helps you develop — that is the professional case for cases.

# THE PEDAGOGIC CASE FOR CASES

Bloom (1956) developed a taxonomy of educational objectives, which is summarized in Figure 1.1. This taxonomy reflects a hierarchy of cognitive skills that people develop as they gain competency in a field. It ranges from simple factual knowledge to the ability to make complex evaluations of circumstances in order to understand how knowledge can be used. It is often used by professors to ensure that exam questions focus on the right level of understanding for the material presented. It also provides a way to test the depth of your own understanding of a field.

In many accounting courses the focus is on the first three levels of this hierarchy — knowledge, comprehension, and application. With these skills you will understand accounting concepts and be able to apply them when provided with structured inputs. For example, if you are told that straight-line amortization (depreciation) is calculated as the purchase price of an asset less the salvage value divided by the asset's useful life (and comprehend the meaning of each of these terms), you will be able to calculate the amount of amortization expense that should be recognized in a given year whenever you are given these values. But this level of understanding doesn't help you explain why amortization expense is used, whether straight-line amortization is the correct approach in a given situation, or how alternative methods of amortization might affect loan covenants or the firm's tax liability. These questions require Bloom's higher levels of understanding — analysis, synthesis, and evaluation.

A traditional, lecture-based accounting course is not designed to develop these higher levels of understanding and ultimately leaves you unprepared for the complexities of financial reporting. If your course stops at that level of understanding, you will be able to prepare or analyze accounting reports under the supervision of others but you will not have developed the competencies to act as an independent professional. Case analyses and discussions are intended to develop your professional and business analysis skills and to provide you with experience in the following:

- Identifying relevant information in complex circumstances based on theoretical models and frameworks;
- Applying analytical models to diagnose and understand causes and consequences;
- Developing group skills, including an appreciation for alternative points of view;
- Solving problems and generating realistic alternative courses of action;
- Making decisions and applying criteria in making choices;
- Justifying recommendations based on evidence, logic, and authoritative guidance; and
- Communicating analyses and conclusions to others.

This case book provides realistic snapshots of business practice and allows you to practise, in the classroom and in group discussions, skills you will be using in your working life. Many of the cases are based on situations that were reported in depth in the financial press and represent decisions — often profoundly important ones — faced by managers, auditors, and investors. The cases encompass a range of businesses

**FIGURE 1.1:** Bloom's Taxonomy of Educational Objectives

| Competence | Skills Demonstrated |
| --- | --- |
| Knowledge | observation and recall of information; knowledge of dates, events, and places; knowledge of major ideas; mastery of subject matter |
| | **Question Cues:** list, define, tell, describe, identify, show, label, collect, examine, tabulate, quote, name, who, when, where, etc. |
| Comprehension | understand information; grasp meaning; translate knowledge into new context; interpret facts; compare and contrast; order and group; infer causes; predict consequences |
| | **Question Cues:** summarize, describe, interpret, contrast, predict, associate, distinguish, estimate, differentiate, discuss, extend |
| Application | use information, methods, concepts, and theories in new situations; solve problems using required skills or knowledge |
| | **Questions Cues:** apply, demonstrate, calculate, complete, illustrate, show, solve, examine, modify, relate, change, classify, experiment, discover |
| Analysis | see patterns; organize parts; recognize hidden meanings; identify components |
| | **Question Cues:** analyze, separate, order, explain, connect, classify, arrange, divide, compare, select, explain, infer |
| Synthesis | use old ideas to create new ones; generalize from given facts; relate knowledge from several areas; predict; draw conclusions |
| | **Question Cues:** combine, integrate, modify, rearrange, substitute, plan, create, design, invent, "what if?", compose, formulate, prepare, generalize, rewrite |
| Evaluation | compare and discriminate between ideas; assess value of theories; make presentations; make choices based on reasoned argument; verify value of evidence; recognize subjectivity |
| | **Question Cues:** assess, decide, rank, grade, test, measure, recommend, convince, select, judge, explain, discriminate, support, conclude, compare, summarize |

Source: Adapted from B.S. Bloom (ed.) (1956), *Taxonomy of Educational Objectives: The Classification of Educational Goals. Handbook I: Cognitive Domain.* New York and Toronto: Longmans, Green.

This version was assembled by Counselling Services at the University of Victoria, Canada. [http://www.coun.uvic.ca/learn/program/hndouts/bloom.html]

including small, family-owned enterprises, medium-sized businesses, and large corporations. This reflects the real-world environment that will be faced by the graduates of top business and accounting programs.

It is important to recognize, however, that the cases in this book may be different from others you have seen. Many "cases" you encounter in textbooks are not really cases in the sense that we use the term here. It has become common to include "cases" as part of the end-of-chapter questions in accounting textbooks, but often these are really just disguised problems rather than true cases. What's the difference? A disguised problem is typically a numerical question where the information that is needed to do the calculation is embedded in a description of the company, its environment, and the particular decision to be made. While you have to do some work to identify the information you need to "solve" the case, ultimately the problem is structured so that there is only one possible answer, which can be calculated with the information given.

Real business decisions are rarely so well defined. Managers must make decisions every day when faced with uncertainties and a number of reasonable alternatives. The mark of an exceptional manager is how well he or she handles these types of decisions. The "case method," as pioneered by the Harvard Business School and now used in many business schools around the world, was developed to provide students with opportunities to practise these skills in the classroom. This style of case was modelled on the "clinical rounds" used in medical education (where students accompany an experienced practitioner and examine real patients) and the "moot courts" used in legal education (where students take on the role of judge, prosecutor, or defender and reargue classic legal cases). A good case discussion at a business school should allow you to practise the diagnostic skills of a clinician and the rhetorical skills of a lawyer.

The cases in this book are based on Harvard's approach, but with a difference. The typical Harvard case is anywhere from ten to ninety pages long and is meant to provide a rich and challenging setting where *experienced* managers can refine their decision-making skills. Harvard cases are designed for graduate education; they are intended for experienced managers who have returned to school to improve their management skills. In order to analyze these cases you need some background knowledge and the basic skills of a practising manager. Each case requires hours of preparation followed by a full class for discussion.

The cases in this book are designed to provide an entrée into the analysis of more complex materials. Each case is short — typically only a few pages long. Though each contains multiple issues, they are not as complex as the Harvard-style full teaching cases. The ones in this book can be read quickly and allow you to practise your case skills in simpler settings. They are designed so that you can use them as a supplement to lectures in order to test your technical knowledge in a decision-making context. You will be able to identify alternatives, consider their consequences, and make recommendations. As you work your way through the cases in this book, your abilities and your confidence in handling more complex problems will increase.

# THE PROFESSIONAL CASE FOR CASES

More and more professional accounting associations and associations of financial analysts and management consultants are encouraging their members to develop case analysis skills; they are also testing their members for those skills. These groups now recognize that knowledge in and of itself is an insufficient basis for developing as a successful practitioner. A professional must have a set of competencies that include the skills to recognize when techniques should be applied, when our existing knowledge may not apply, and when a new approach might better achieve clients' and society's objectives.

The CFA Institute, for its Chartered Financial Analyst (CFA) designation, uses Bloom's taxonomy to organize its three-level examination structure, the purpose of which is to certify the competence of investment professionals. "At Level I, candidates are asked basic knowledge and comprehension questions and are asked to perform some analysis. At Level II, the focus is on analysis and application; at Level III, the focus is on synthesis and integration."[1] The body of knowledge that CFAs must acquire includes knowledge of financial statement analysis. In particular, the "candidate should be able to i) analyze and use financial statements and accompanying disclosures in the investment valuation process; ii) analyze a company's liquidity, profitability, financial stability, solvency, and asset utilization; and iii) analyze the effects of alternative accounting methods and assumptions on financial statements."[2] This last point recognizes that management has made choices and assumptions that will affect the reported financial information. Financial analysts and investors must be able to understand how these choices will affect how they use the information.

All of Canada's professional accounting bodies now test candidates for their case analysis skills. The Canadian Institute of Chartered Accountants (CICA), for example, uses a uniform evaluation process (UFE) to test candidates for the CA designation. This examination "will challenge you to demonstrate your competence by responding to simulations/business scenarios that represent the kinds of challenges you have faced during your work experience, or will soon be facing in your professional career as a CA."[3] The Certified General Accountants of Canada (CGA) have designed their education program to "develop the abilities to analyze and interpret financial information; the skills to think creatively and to solve complex problems; the expertise to plan, forecast, and implement corporate strategies; and to communicate effectively."[4] Similarly, the Society of Certified Management Accountants (CMA) uses a series of case-based assessments to provide "a forum for candidates to demonstrate their ability to think strategically and effectively manage complex issues within an integrative

---

[1] Robert Johnson, "Preparing for the CFA Exam," *Professional Investor,* February 2004, pp. 30–31.

[2] http://www.cfainstitute.org/cfaprogram/pdf/studyguides06/Level_II.Final.FSA.pdf

[3] http://www.cica.ca/index.cfm/ci_id/610/la_id/1.htm. Accessed January 21, 2005.

[4] http://www.cga-ontario.org/newfiles/becoming04/why/why.htm. Accessed January 21, 2005.

framework."[5] Each of these professional associations has recognized that case analysis skills constitute a core competency for professional accountants.

In the United States, the American Institute of Certified Public Accountants (AICPA) *Vision Project*[6] has identified the following as the five core competencies of CPAs:

- **Communications and Leadership Skills** — Able to give and exchange information within meaningful context and with appropriate delivery and interpersonal skills. Able to influence, inspire, and motivate others to achieve results.
- **Strategic and Critical Thinking Skills** — Able to link data, knowledge, and insight together to provide quality advice for strategic decision-making.
- **Focus on the Customer, Client and Market** — Able to anticipate and meet the changing needs of clients, employers, customers, and markets better than competitors.
- **Interpretation of Converging Information** — Able to interpret and provide a broader context using financial and non-financial information.
- **Technologically Adept** — Able to utilize and leverage technology in ways that add value to clients, customers and employers.

This list of core competencies again captures the key skills that case analysis requires — in particular, the ability to interpret complex information, to apply strategic and critical thinking skills, and to communicate effectively with clients and peers.

Whichever designation you hope to attain, whichever country you want to practise in, and whether you will be preparing or auditing financial statements or using financial statements to make investment decisions, the public expectations of professional accountants, managers, and investment analysts are the same. You must be able to analyze complex information, develop alternatives, provide recommendations, and show how your recommendations can be implemented. These are the skills you will develop as you use this book.

---

[5] http://www.cma-canada.org/multimedia/CMA_Canada/Document_Library/Attachments/ leadership-booklet.pdf. Accessed January 21, 2005.

[6] http://www.aicpa.org/vision/index.htm. Accessed January 21, 2005.

# C H A P T E R  2

# PRINCIPLED JUDGMENT IN FINANCIAL REPORTING

"Judgment pervades accounting and auditing. It is exercised in considering whether the substance of transactions differs from their form, in resolving questions of materiality and adequacy of disclosure, in deciding whether an estimate can be made of the effects of future events on current financial statements, and in allocating receipts and expenditures over time and among activities." *The Commission on Auditors' Responsibilities Report,* "Conclusions and Recommendations" (New York 1978, p. 16)

By its very nature, financial reporting requires the use of judgment by managers, financial accountants, and auditors.[1] Financial reports reduce complex business transactions to a few summary statistics; thousands of individual sales transactions, for example, are reported as a single revenue number on the income statement. When data are summarized in this way, choices must be made. These choices are in part technical — that is, they are alternative ways of representing the same concept in much the same way that either the mean, the mode, or the median can be used to summarize the central tendency of a distribution. These choices are also political in the sense that financial reports are used to make decisions; thus the information they contain can affect how resources are allocated in society. Financial reports are also used to evaluate the performance of managers and companies. At the risk of sounding melodramatic, people's lives are affected by how financial reports capture and communicate what a company has done.

The cases in this book provide you with practice at making choices that will shape financial statements. For those of you who will be helping prepare financial statements as managers, accountants, or auditors, these skills will be crucial to your role in managing the company's communications with various stakeholders. For those of you who will be analyzing financial statements as financial analysts, investment bankers, or portfolio managers, these skills will allow you to better understand what financial

---

[1] See G.A. Brown, R. Collins, and D.B. Thornton, "Professional Judgment and Accounting Standards," *Accounting, Organizations and Society* 18(4) (May 1993), pp. 275–289.

statements really say and how the choices made by management have affected the numbers you are using in your decisions.

Judgment and choice are key elements in the preparation of financial statements, but this does not imply that "anything goes." Financial statements are constrained by legal requirements, professional norms, and conceptual principles, all of which place limits on how a company can present itself through its financial statements. Because financial statements are used to communicate with key stakeholders, managers are also guided in their choices by the purposes to which the financial statements will be put. In this chapter we explore these constraints and the strategic questions that you must consider when exercising judgment in financial reporting.[2]

## GAAP AND FINANCIAL STATEMENTS

The financial reports that are most visible in our society are those produced by publicly traded companies and included with their annual reports to shareholders. These financial statements are usually produced in accordance with generally accepted accounting principles (GAAP). In Canada, most provincial and federal laws that require companies to produce financial statements define GAAP as the contents of the *CICA Handbook* (hereafter "the Handbook"). The Handbook defines GAAP as "the conventions, rules and procedures that determine accepted accounting practices at a particular time." In other words, GAAP is more than a single document or set of rules; it is constantly changing and, furthermore, it is different for different circumstances. GAAP represents our current consensus on how large companies should report to their shareholders.

An important part of GAAP is the accounting standards that have been generated by various standard-setting bodies. In the United States the Financial Accounting Standards Board (FASB) is the key source for the accounting standards used when structuring financial reports. The equivalent body in Canada is the Accounting Standards Board (AcSB). For many years, Canadian GAAP and American GAAP reflected different styles of standard setting. The United States was known for creating detailed rules for measurement and disclosure that were intended to cover every conceivable transaction in which a company might engage. Canada was known for standards that emphasized general principles and for allowing professional judgment in the implementation of those principles.[3] There are signs that American GAAP and Canadian GAAP are converging. In 2005 the AcSB released a draft strategic plan that called for the adoption of international financial reporting standards (IFRS) in Canada within five years. These standards are developed by the International Accounting Standards Board (IASB), an international body composed of technical experts from various

---

[2] The material in this chapter is complementary to the coverage of the qualitative characteristics of financial information (e.g., decision usefulness, relevance, reliability, timeliness, verifiability) covered in most textbooks. Our focus is on the choices that must be made among alternatives that would meet these qualitative criteria.

[3] We will return to this issue in the last section of this chapter.

regions of the developed world. FASB is also working to harmonize its standards with the IFRS, having been explicitly directed to do so by the U.S. Securities and Exchange Commission (SEC). It appears increasingly likely that there will be convergence among the major industrialized countries — that IFRS will eventually become GAAP for large companies.

One purpose of accounting standards is to provide guidance for the exercise of judgment by managers, financial accountants, and auditors. Accounting standards attempt to ensure that similar events are reported in similar ways by different companies. The convergence on IFRS by the United States and Canada reflects a consensus among standard setters that accounting standards should be "principles-based" — that is, that they should be general statements rather than specific rules, and designed to support general-purpose financial statements that can be used by investors, employees, lenders, suppliers, customers, governments, and the public. Both these characteristics build the need for judgment into the financial reporting process.

The focus on principles means that the specific approach to reporting must be chosen to fit the circumstances instead of simply to comply with detailed rules. Furthermore, management has a responsibility to ensure that the choice of accounting policies does not result in materially misleading financial statements. A principles-based approach calls on management to focus on the social purpose of financial reporting and to ensure that the choices of accounting policies made serve those broad objectives. The decision by regulators to encourage a principles-based approach to preparing financial reports is, in part, motivated by their belief that this will result in information that is of greater value to users.

Creating general-purpose financial statements to serve multiple users (instead of producing different financial statements tailored to the needs of various user groups) also means that managers must choose between alternative ways of reporting the company's financial performance. Standard setters have tried to reduce the degree of choice by emphasizing that financial reports should provide information that is useful for both current and potential shareholders when they are making economic decisions. This implies that at a minimum, financial statements must specify clearly the resources available to the organization, the claims on those resources, and the organization's ability to generate future cash inflows.[4]

The convergence on IFRS as a basis for American and Canadian GAAP means that Canada will allow managers to exercise less judgment than before when interpreting standards; at the same time, American standards will become less rule-oriented. The convergence is towards what we call "principled judgment" — that is, judgment guided and constrained by agreement on what general-purpose financial statements should achieve and on what the legitimate alternatives are for achieving those objectives. No set of standards can remove the need for judgment in summarizing complex information designed for multiple users, but guidelines or principles can focus the decisions that must be made.

---

[4] See H.G. Bullen and K. Crook, "Revisiting the Concepts: A New Conceptual Framework Project," FASB/IASB, May 2005.

Examine the statement (reproduced below) that Bell Canada Enterprises (BCE) included in its 2004 annual report to shareholders.[5] Note how that company's managers acknowledged the judgments they made in preparing the financial statements and the criteria they used in making those judgments.

> The financial statements and all of the information in this annual report are the responsibility of the management of BCE Inc. and have been reviewed and approved by the board of directors. The board of directors is responsible for ensuring that management fulfills its financial reporting responsibilities. Deloitte & Touche LLP, the shareholders' auditors, have audited the financial statements.
>
> Management has prepared the financial statements according to Canadian generally accepted accounting principles. Under these principles, management has made certain estimates and assumptions that are reflected in the financial statements and notes. Management believes that these financial statements fairly present BCE's consolidated financial position, results of operations and cash flows."

## NON-GAAP FINANCIAL STATEMENTS

It is important to recognize that not all financial statements are subject to GAAP. Most laws that constrain financial reporting are designed to protect the shareholders of publicly traded, widely held[6] corporations (e.g., firms such as BCE); for these people, annual reports and the accompanying financial statements provide the key information on which they base their assessments of management as well as their decisions to hold or sell their shares. But much of Canada's economic activity is generated by small organizations; in fact, 99.9 percent of Canadian businesses employ fewer than five hundred people.[7] An entity of this size may operate as:

- a sole proprietorship (an unincorporated business with a single owner who is personally liable for the debts of the business);
- a partnership (a business owned by a small number of owners based on a contract between them);
- a private corporation (an incorporated business without publicly traded shares); *or*
- a not-for-profit entity (an entity that cannot distribute dividends or sell shares and that typically operates to serve some social purpose).

---

[5] http://www.bce.ca/en/investors/reports/annual/bce/2004annual/bce_ar04_02.php.

[6] The term "widely held" means that there are many shareholders, each holding a small percentage of the company's shares.

[7] http://strategis.ic.gc.ca/epic/internet/insbrp-rppe.nsf/en/rd00009e.html. Accessed July 29, 2005.

The financial reports of these entities may be more informative for specific uses and users if they vary from GAAP in certain respects.[8] For example, a partnership may use financial reports to decide how to split the income of the business among partners. The definition of income under GAAP may not be the one the partners have chosen for their own purposes. Similarly, a bank may ask a small business to provide non-GAAP financial statements prepared according to its own preferences for accounting policies that focus on cash flow. In these situations the choice of accounting policies will be directed by the specific use that will be made of the financial statements.

Some companies prefer to provide investors with non-GAAP performance measures *in addition to* their regular financial statements that are prepared according to GAAP. For example, Transat, a company that specializes in holiday travel packages, provides investors with several non-GAAP measures of performance, which it uses itself to manage the business.[9]

> Transat prepares its financial statements in accordance with Canadian generally accepted accounting principles ("GAAP"). The Corporation will occasionally refer to non-GAAP financial measures in the news release [three of these measures are defined below]. These non-GAAP financial measures do not have any meaning prescribed by GAAP and are therefore unlikely to be comparable to similar measures presented by other issuers. They are furnished to provide additional information and should not be considered as a substitute for measures of performance prepared in accordance with GAAP.
>
> [Non-GAAP Performance measured used by Transat include:]
>
> (1) Revenues less operating expenses (non-GAAP financial measure used by management as an indicator to evaluate ongoing and recurring operational performance).
> (2) Debt plus off-balance sheet arrangements (non-GAAP financial measure used by management to assess the Corporation's future liquidity requirements).
> (3) Total debt less cash and cash equivalents not in trust or otherwise reserved (non-GAAP financial measure used by management to assess its liquidity position).

Again, in circumstances such as these, management has broad discretion regarding what is reported and what form those disclosures take. Any user of these statements must consider how the information has been developed and whether the disclosures are useful to them as presented.

---

[8] This is recognized in Canada through the "differential reporting" principle in Section 1300 of the Handbook.

[9] http://www.transat.com/en/media_centre/2.0.media.centre.asp?id=876.

# THINGS TO CONSIDER WHEN EXERCISING JUDGMENT IN FINANCIAL REPORTING

Since the need for judgment pervades financial reporting, the question becomes this: What things must we consider in order to provide good financial reports? The financial reporting process has been described as a value chain in which different actors contribute to the value of financial reports.[10] The participants in this value chain include financial report preparers (managers, financial accountants), those who exercise oversight (the board of directors, the audit committee, the auditor, the regulators), and the users of financial statements (current shareholders, creditors, unions, financial analysts, investors, etc.). Each person in this value chain has a responsibility to examine the financial reports and consider whether the choices made have resulted in financial reporting of the required quality. Although their needs and perspectives may differ, each person in the financial reporting value chain must ask these questions: Who are the users of the financial statements? What are their information needs? What legal and ethical constraints affect the company's financial reports? What estimates and assumptions were used to generate the numbers? Was the information presented in such a way as to facilitate its use?

## WHO ARE THE USERS?

Financial reporting is an attempt to provide a wide variety of users with the information they need to make decisions and hold management accountable (this definition encompasses both investment and stewardship uses of information). So the first question you should ask if you are recommending an approach to financial reporting (or analyzing a case) is this: Who will be using the financial reports, and for what purpose? Different decision makers will require different information. For example, the information required by a bank to determine whether it should approve a loan to a company is different from that of a tax agency deciding on the amount of income tax the company owes the government. Because financial reports often have multiple users, the potentially conflicting information needs of many groups have to be taken into account when deciding on their content and form.

Besides identifying the users and the types of decisions they will make with the financial information, you should also consider whether the users will have preferences that may generate pressure to "tilt" the information in certain directions. For example, in a private company, if management is rewarded based on accounting measures of performance, managers have an incentive to make choices that increase the reported income of the firm; however, this may conflict with the current shareholders' preference, which is to minimize reported income in order to minimize tax liabilities. If a bank uses financial statements to assess the value of assets (e.g., inventories) that have been pledged as collateral to secure a loan, it will want to ensure that the value

---

10 S.A. DiPiazza and R.G. Eccles. *Building Public Trust: The Future of Corporate Reporting.* New York: Wiley, 2002.

of the asset is conservatively stated; by contrast, the company's management may prefer an optimistic valuation method. These types of conflicts are common in financial reporting.

By thinking through the information needs of users and how management may respond to the incentives to report in different ways, you will achieve a better understanding of the forces that shape the content and form of financial reports.

## WHAT ESTIMATES AND ASSUMPTIONS ARE NEEDED TO CALCULATE ACCRUALS?

The most basic reason why financial reporting requires managers to exercise judgment is the use of "accrual accounting." Accrual accounting attempts to report the effects of management decisions or transactions in the periods they affect, regardless of the timing of the cash flows associated with those decisions. For example, the decision to purchase a new machine (or other long-lived asset) will have consequences for the company for many years into the future. Instead of just recording the cost of that new machine as an expense at the time of purchase, we capitalize its cost and use amortization to match its cost with the benefits received from it in future periods. Accrual accounting requires managers to make forecasts about future events and build these forecasts into their accounting accruals. In the case of a new machine, for example, in order to calculate an amortization expense we must estimate its useful life, taking into account possible technological changes, wear and tear, and the effort required to maintain it. We also need to decide which costs are legitimately parts of the asset base we are amortizing. For example, should we include the cost of searching for the new machine, the cost of installing it, and the cost of training workers to use it? So any time there is an accrual, questions arise as to whether the estimates are both fair and based on reasonable assumptions. Many accounting standards attempt to place boundaries around the approach to accruals that managers may use.

Consider the news item reproduced in Figure 2.1. Research and development (R&D) expenses are intended by the company to have future value, so should they be treated like an investment in a new machine (and thus reported as an asset that generates future value), or should they instead be treated as an expense when the work is done? It may be that when Ballard Power puts money into R&D (which is expensed, creating a current loss), the market takes this as a signal that some future earnings will be based on the invention or development of saleable products. Here it seems that both the market and those who set accounting standards are contending different things about the future value of Ballard's R&D efforts. There are legitimate debates about how such expenses should be treated and whether managers should be allowed to choose how to report them. This is one area in which standard setters in different countries disagree about how best to account for the economic substance of a transaction and how much discretion management should be allowed to exercise in accounting for its expense.

**FIGURE 2.1:** Ballard Power Accounting Losses

### Ballard Losses Double

Canadian fuel cell developer Ballard Power Systems Inc. said yesterday that its losses almost doubled in the fourth quarter because of accelerated spending on product research.

The company, which has seen its stock price more than triple since January, enjoyed another jump with shares closing at $189, up $14 on the Toronto Stock Exchange.

"We continue to push ahead with an aggressive research and product development program," Ballard said in a statement. Officials later added that R&D spending will increase again this year but at a slower rate.

The Burnaby, B.C.-based Company said it lost $26-million or 31 cents a share in the fourth quarter, compared with a loss of $13.5-million or 16 cents a share a year earlier, before the inclusion of net gains resulting from the issuance of shares by subsidiaries and affiliated companies.

The loss in the final three months of 1999 was 31 cents a share, compared with a loss of 2 cents in the same quarter of 1998.

Revenue more than doubled in the quarter to $14.9-million from $6.6-million as sales from both its automotive and stationary power unit businesses improved. Most of the sales have been to companies researching how to incorporate fuel cells into their products.

Losses for the year climbed to $75.2-million on total revenue of $33.1-million from $36.2-million on revenue of $25.1-million the year before.

Fuel cells generate power electrochemically from energy sources such as hydrogen and have been promoted as a potential replacement for everything from cell phone batteries to the internal combustion automobile engine.

Source: "Ballard Losses Double," *The Globe and Mail,* March 11, 2000, B3.

Questions about the role of estimates and assumptions in financial reporting focus our attention on how we measure the impact of business "transactions" — that is, exchanges between the reporting entity and external parties. But what about the actions companies take that do not involve transactions with other parties? One of the current concerns of critics of the state of financial reporting is that what we report is limited by what the accounting model can recognize and measure. For example, environmental groups have been pushing for the cost of "externalities" to be included in companies' financial reports. Externalities are the costs or benefits of actions that are imposed on others without their consent. When a factory disposes of hazardous materials through its smokestack, it causes health problems, property damage, and environmental damage. The costs of dealing with the problems caused by the disposal of hazardous materials in this way are incurred by third parties (third parties are those who are affected even though they did not enter into a contract with the person creating the harm) or by nature. These are negative externalities of the company's operations. Since we don't measure these costs, the company does not report them and may not include them as factors when deciding on the most cost effective way to deal with hazardous materials. Increasingly, society is looking for ways to internalize these costs — that is, to hold persons or companies responsible for these costs. This can be accomplished through regulation, through the legal system (e.g., civil lawsuits), or by creating a price system for pollution.

One thing to consider when examining a company's financial reports is whether they reflect all of the costs (and benefits) of the company's operations. If they do not, the financial statements may not enable you to thoroughly evaluate the firm and its prospects. Financial statements must always be interpreted in the context of the firm's business model, its physical activities, and the social and environmental context in which it operates. Some users may find that the financial statements do not capture all of the activities of the company that are important to them.

## WHAT LEGAL AND ETHICAL CONSTRAINTS AFFECT THE REPORTS?

The form and content of financial reports is affected by a wide range of constraints. If a company is listed on a public stock exchange, there will be stock exchange rules relating to financial disclosures.[11] Various national and international financial accounting standards may limit how the company can measure and disclose information depending on the jurisdiction in which it operates.[12] Certain types of companies (e.g., financial institutions) face reporting rules specifically included in the legislation that authorizes their creation. The information preparer must identify these constraints and decide whether they apply in the circumstances.

The effect of these constraints on actual practice is variable. The management of the reporting entity must decide whether the constraints are binding — that is, what the consequences of violating the constraints could be for the company. For example, in the United States a survey of company compliance with an accounting standard concerning the disclosure of warranty liabilities[13] found that 20 percent of companies with product warranty programs did not disclose this liability.[14] Some decisions not to comply would have been based on materiality considerations (i.e., the warranty cost was so small it would not have affected decision making); some would have been

---

[11] For example, the TSX requirements can be reviewed at http://www.tse.com/en/productsAndServices/listings/tse/resources/resourceManual.html.

[12] For Canadian standards refer to www.acsbcanada.org and for international standards refer to http://www.iasb.org/standards/summaries.asp.

[13] When a firm guarantees its product, i.e. provides a warranty, it is making a promise to the consumer to fix or replace the product in the future should it prove defective. Under accrual accounting, the company must estimate the cost of this warranty and record it at the time it sells the product since the sale of the product commits the company to this future cost.

[14] See http://www.warrantyweek.com/archive/ww20031229.html. Accessed May 3, 2005.

based on concerns over the effect of releasing proprietary information (e.g., an estimate of the product's reliability) that might provide a competitor with an advantage. Even where legal requirements exist, management must still decide whether to comply with them (and a savvy financial analyst would be aware that certain information was missing from the financial statements and question management about this omission).

In Canada and the United States the managers of publicly listed companies have clear responsibility for the quality of information they provide to shareholders through their financial statements. This is intended to reinforce managers' personal liability for any errors, misleading statements, or omissions in the financial statements. Consider the following statement, from the 2004 financial statements of Sleeman Breweries:

> The accompanying consolidated financial statements were prepared by management, which is responsible for the integrity and fairness of the information presented, including the amounts based on estimates and judgments. These consolidated financial statements were prepared in accordance with Canadian generally accepted accounting principles.
>
> To assist in discharging these responsibilities, management maintains internal controls which are designed to provide reasonable assurance that its assets are safeguarded, that transactions are executed in accordance with management's authorization, and that the financial records form a reliable base for the preparation of accurate and timely financial information.
>
> The Board of Directors oversees management's responsibilities for financial reporting through an Audit Committee which is composed entirely of unrelated directors. This committee reviews the consolidated financial statements of the Company and recommends them to the Board for approval."[15]

This statement identifies several constraints on management's choice of financial reporting policies. Does the requirement to make such a statement constrain management? How would users' reliance on these financial reports be affected by management's statement of responsibility?

Beyond the legal requirements affecting financial disclosure, managers and auditors have an ethical responsibility to provide information to organizational stakeholders that will allow them to exercise their decision-making rights. For example, shareholders need to have valid information about the future earnings potential of the organization and the risks being taken to generate those returns; debt holders will have concerns about the liquidity and solvency of the organization (i.e., Will the company be able to repay a loan when it becomes due?); governments require financial information to provide a basis for fair taxation, appropriate regulation, and the protection of third parties; unions are concerned about the fairness of wages and the stability of employment for their members. The ethical implications of disclosure and measurement choices must be considered by those who prepare and audit financial reports.

15 http://www.sleeman.com/LinkManager/pdfs/Sleeman_English_Annual_sm.pdf.

Many companies now provide an explicit code of ethics for their senior managers. This is intended to ensure that everyone understands the company's core values and how they should be implemented and will be enforced. All professional accounting associations require that their members exercise their responsibilities with due diligence and ethical sensitivity. Remember that many senior managers have accounting designations and so are subject to these codes of ethics even if they are not practising accountants. These codes of ethics involve two key dimensions: the need to maintain independence of mind when making decisions or giving advice, and the need to act in the public interest.

Professional codes of ethics usually include guidelines for identifying situations where either a professional's ability to provide objective, unbiased, and independent advice would be impaired ("independence in fact"), or a reasonable person might assume that conditions would impair the professional's independence ("independence in appearance"). The value of a professional's advice to a client and the value of a manager's decision-making authority are both increased when their judgment is unimpaired.[16] Professional independence does not mean you do not care about your client or your organization; it does mean that you do not simply tell people what they want to hear and that you do not base your advice on your own interests. The exercise of judgment must be based on the facts of the case, on your knowledge and logic, and (in some cases) on your own character, which must be strong enough that you are ready to give your opinion in the face of opposition.

Although most professionals deal with a particular client or employer, society also expects professionals to act in the public interest. There is great debate about what "the public interest" means in accounting and other professions. At a minimum, the "public interest" is a way of recognizing that multiple stakeholders are affected by a professional's decisions. For example, a physician may want to prescribe an antibiotic for a patient but may also know that the improper use or overuse of antibiotics has resulted in the evolution of drug-resistant strains of bacteria, which create a wider risk to society. The physician has to balance the immediate needs of a particular patient against the long-term health of the population. Similarly, financial reporting that provides a temporary advantage to one company but undermines the public's trust in capital markets would violate the public interest.

The "public interest" has also been used in reference to certain common values that society recognizes as being more important than individual short-term gain. When a client asks a professional to use his/her skills to advance an illegal, immoral, or unethical objective, that professional is expected to refuse the assignment. This expectation is based on the idea that a professional is also a member of society and must act in that context. The existence of an ethical dilemma (i.e., a conflict between users or between different expectations) should be recognized and a deliberate choice made about how to handle it.

---

[16] Note that "independence of mind" is not assured by "independence in appearance" or "independence in fact." While we strive for independence of mind, all that can be observed by others is independence in appearance and independence in fact.

As we have discussed, financial accounting standards are converging on a principles-based approach to financial reporting. This approach requires judgment skills; it also emphasizes the importance of recognizing and resolving ethical dilemmas in financial reporting. Under a principles-based approach to financial reporting, it is not enough to say that the rules allow you to report transactions in a particular way — you must also consider whether the financial report is consistent with the principles and the objectives of those who will use the information. When adherence to a rule would violate the principle, all members of the financial reporting value chain are obliged to ensure that the principle is honoured.

## HOW SHOULD THE INFORMATION BE REPORTED?

Once we have decided to recognize and measure the consequences of a transaction, the next choice concerns whether and how to disclose that information. This is tied to the first issue discussed earlier: Who are the users of the information, and what decisions will they make based on that information?

Much of the discussion of this subject has focused on investors and on whether or not stock prices fairly reflect the value of the company based on the available information. Most of those who set accounting standards recognize present and future investors as key users of general-purpose financial reports. How management must release information to these users depends on the "efficiency" with which the markets process information. Fama (1965) describes an efficient market as follows:

> In an efficient market, competition among the many intelligent participants leads to a situation where, at any point in time, actual prices of individual securities already reflect the effects of information based both on events that have already occurred and on events which, as of now, the market expects to take place in the future. In other words, in an efficient market at any point in time the actual price of a security will be a good estimate of its intrinsic value.[17]

Fama (1970) also distinguishes among three forms of efficiency:

- Weak-form efficiency — where the market reacts to past prices only;
- Semistrong-form efficiency — where the market reacts to all publicly available information; *and*
- Strong-form efficiency — where the market reflects the information known to any market participant.

There is plenty of evidence that markets are more than weak-form efficient. Market prices react to the release of new information about the future earnings

---

[17] E. Fama, "Random Walks in Stock Price Behaviour." Special Paper 16, School of Business, University of Chicago, 1965, p. 4; Eugene F. Fama, "Efficient Capital Markets: A Review of Theory and Empirical Work," *Journal of Finance,* Volume 25, Issue 2, Papers and Proceedings of the Twenty-Eighth Annual Meeting of the American Finance Association, New York, N.Y. December, 28–30, 1969 (May 1970), 383–417.

prospects or costs of a firm and not just to the history of past trades in a security. But the difference between strong-form and semistrong-form efficiency has significant implications for financial disclosure.

In a strong-form efficient market, it does not matter to the market's overall efficiency whether we disclose information through financial statements, but this will affect who gains and loses. In this type of market even private information is reflected in market prices, so there is no need to require any specific financial disclosures. Note that strong-form efficiency simply means that the person with better information is able to trade on it until the prices reflect the value of that information. For example, it has been argued that insider trading (e.g., management buying and selling shares in their own company based on their private knowledge of company plans or results) is an effective way to ensure that market prices reflect everything that is known about a firm. Others argue, however, that this is achieved at a cost to the average investor, who can be duped into selling or buying shares based on incomplete information. Some would argue that this is ethically wrong and that it will ultimately lead to the average investor refusing to participate in the capital markets. Our approach to financial reporting is not based on this model of efficient markets.

If the capital market is semistrong-form efficient, *how* we disclose information is not important as long as the information is released. This version of market efficiency is consistent with most studies of the capital market's reaction to accounting information. The market seems able to handle different formats of information equally well and is not fooled when different accounting policies are used to report events — provided the policies are disclosed along with the information. This form of market efficiency, however, means that the choice of *what* we release is very important and that people can gain by acting on private information. This model of market efficiency suggests that we need rules to control insider trading and that rules specifying what must be disclosed are more important than rules specifying how things should be measured. This model of market efficiency is consistent with most recent approaches to the setting of accounting standards.

The concern with market efficiency for the most part ignores the distributional effects of choices about information disclosure — that is, how information can allow some to gain at the expense of others. Even though tests of market efficiency suggest that on average, market prices reflect new information in an unbiased way, studies of individual decision makers indicate that people do make systematic mistakes depending on how information is framed. More important, there is evidence that how information is presented does have an impact on contract negotiations and on other nonmarket uses of accounting information. In part this result is because these settings deal with small numbers of people and transactions, where mistakes do not "average out" as they might in a market setting. Also in part this result reflects a bargaining context where information is used strategically to accomplish specific objectives. These concerns should be taken into account when deciding on a financial reporting strategy.

A final issue concerns transaction costs — that is, the costs of providing the information to users. Although a market may process information in a strong-form or semistrong-form efficient manner, this does not tell us the most cost-efficient way to release information. Transaction-cost efficiency requires that the information needed to allow markets to be allocatively efficient[18] be released in the most cost-efficient way. For example, to consider an extreme case, would it be more efficient for each investor to call the company and ask for the information he or she needs in order to decide whether to invest in the company? Or should the company release the information publicly to all investors? Obviously, it is more cost efficient for the company to provide an annual report instead of dealing with each investor individually. The current push for real-time, online financial reports is based largely on the argument that this will reduce the cost of achieving efficient capital markets.

Also, there are transaction-cost implications in a firm's choice of accounting policies and in a country's choice of standard-setting regime. The market may be able to correctly price firms' securities based on financial reporting under either IFRS or American GAAP, but investors still face the cost of restating companies' financial statements on a consistent basis in order to make decisions. Similarly, when different companies in the same industry choose different accounting policies, investors comparing companies bear the costs of adjusting these reports to a consistent basis.

The current debates about the regulation of financial reporting are rooted in two implicit assumptions: that markets are only semistrongly efficient (and hence disclosure matters); and that the distributional consequences of financial reporting are important (and hence who knows what and when is important). Decisions whether and how to disclose financial information within the framework presented above are made by asking three questions: (1) Does some stakeholder have a legitimate right to information necessary to make a decision regarding the firm? (2) Will the lack of disclosure result in unfair enrichment of those who possess the information? (3) What is the most cost-effective way to provide the information needed? Answering these questions will help you decide how best to disclose financial information.

## STANDARDS FOR FINANCIAL REPORTING: RULES VERSUS PRINCIPLES

We noted earlier in this chapter that accounting standard-setting is converging on a "principles-based" approach. Canada and the United Kingdom have used this approach for many years. In the wake of the failure of Enron, the United States has decided that this approach is less subject to abuse[19] than a rules-based approach; thus it is moving its standard-setting approach in this direction. The IASB has also committed to a principles-based approach to accounting standards, and its standards, the IFRS, have become the focus of efforts to harmonize accounting standards across

---

[18] Allocative efficiency means that the price of a security reflects its underlying value, i.e. that it is fairly priced compared with other assets.

[19] Management may find ways to construct transactions or choose accounting policies that comply with the rule but effectively undermine what the rule was trying to prevent.

borders. This convergence, however, is not happening easily, and there are strong advocates of a rules-based approach to standard setting.

In the regulation of economic affairs there is constant tension between two approaches. On one side the argument is made that we need clear and unambiguous rules so that we can arrange our business affairs and know that if we cross the line our behaviour will be regarded as inappropriate, unethical, and/or illegal. A rules-based approach means that everyone is treated the same and that there is an objective standard that guides and evaluates behaviour. On the other side the argument is made that it is impossible to anticipate every circumstance and to create rules that apply in all situations. In this dynamic world, new transactions are invented every day, and the conduct of business must be based on a set of principles that can be applied to any new circumstance that arises. Principles allow for variations; they allow us to treat each situation according to its unique nature and liberate us from the assumption that "one size fits all." A principles-based approach attempts to reflect the values on which society is based rather than the behaviours it prohibits at a particular point in time.

In accounting it has been argued that a rules-based approach means that managers and auditors are able to ensure that they are in compliance with the law; some of the risk of being accused of improper financial disclosure is thereby reduced. For example, when investors believe they have been misled by the financial statements of a company they may sue management for misleading them and sue the auditor for allowing the misstatement to appear in the financial statements. Managers and auditors want to be able to defend themselves by providing evidence that their disclosures and audits complied with the rules.

One of the downsides of a rules-based system is that company managers may have an incentive to come as close to breaking the rules as possible in order to accomplish their ends. Those managers may be trying to meet investors' expectations for profit, or they may be trying to meet profit targets in order to receive bonuses. The attitude becomes "Where does it say I can't do that?" rather than "Is it the right thing to do?" In some situations meeting the letter of the law results in significant violations of the spirit of the law. When Enron failed, for example, it became evident that it was able to disguise what it was doing in part by creating "special-purpose entities"[20] (more than three thousand of them), which, depending on the level of outside ownership, did not need to be integrated into its consolidated balance sheet. To put it simply, Enron was able to hide the level of debt it was incurring and exaggerate its revenues by applying a set of rules in a way that regulators had not anticipated.

In a rules-based environment the key problem for accountants and auditors is how to determine which rule applies to a given transaction and report the transaction within the limits of that rule. Showing that the choice of financial disclosure method is consistent with the rule provides an end to the process. In a principles-based environment the key problem is how to implement the general principle in a given situation. Here, however, the choice of how to disclose financial transactions must advance

---

[20] A "special-purpose entity" is a company created by another company to fulfil a temporary or "special" role.

**FIGURE 2.2:** The Letter versus the Spirit (KPMG Discussion Series)

There is one thing everyone agrees on. The U.S. rules-based accounting approach is not working as well as it should. Something has to change. But first we need to carefully weigh the merits of alternative approaches.

Proponents of rules-based accounting claim that the fewer the rules, the greater the potential for confusion. If rules are replaced with principles, those responsible for reporting will adhere to subjective interpretations, and investors will be left without a common measuring stick with which to compare financial statements, or worse, with a misleading portrayal of a company's financial picture.

On the other hand, proponents of principles-based accounting claim the real issue is a matter of substance over form. Rules may lay out exactly what to do, but they can also provide a roadmap that lays out what to do to get around them whereas a principles-based approach focuses on the spirit of the underlying standard.

While each side raises valid points, there is a strong argument for a principles-based approach, which would allow U.S. accounting practices to more readily converge with global standards. However, any effective accounting model guided by principles must be supported by rules that create boundaries leading to consistency.

Under this model, regulators will need to accept judgment, and not "second-guess" when reasonable judgment is used. Moreover, any shift towards principles-based accounting suggests a need to revisit U.S. tort liability.

Overall, a principles-based approach could help the auditing profession and public companies deliver more comprehensive, intuitive and transparent financial information.

Understanding the need to revisit the approach used to govern financial statements can be beneficial for everyone: businesses, the auditing profession and, most importantly, the investor.

Source: The Partners and Professionals of KPMG LLP

the objectives of that process — the substance is more important than the form. Regardless of the environment in which you operate, the problem remains the same: How do we measure and disclose the consequences of a given transaction? The difference is our starting point and the social consequences of our choices.

The discussion of rules-based versus principles-based accounting by KPMG reproduced in Figure 2.2 brings out some of the issues and complexities. There is a fear among many that the change to a principles-based approach will require judgments that will be challenged in courts of law. KPMG is calling for a change in the law to ensure that if good faith judgment is exercised, managers and auditors will be protected from legal liability.

After the failure of Enron, the U.S. Congress directed the SEC — under Section 108(d) of the *Sarbanes-Oxley Act* of 2002 — to consider a principles-based approach to accounting standards. This mandate in turn was passed on to the FASB, which produces accounting standards on behalf of the SEC. A staff study has recommended that "objectives-based" accounting standards[21] be developed with the following characteristics:

- Be based on an improved and consistently applied conceptual framework;
- Clearly state the accounting objective of the standard;
- Provide sufficient detail and structure so that the standard can be operationalized and applied on a consistent basis;
- Minimize the use of exceptions from the standard;
- Avoid use of percentage tests ("bright-lines") that allow financial engineers to achieve technical compliance with the standard while evading the intent of the standard.

The challenge is for the FASB to implement this mandate and, more importantly, for universities, colleges, and professional associations that train managers and accountants to move their programs from a rules-based to a principles-based approach.

In Canada the AcSB has released a draft strategic plan that calls for the harmonization of Canadian accounting standards with IFRS (produced by the IASB). This represents a marked departure from AcSB's previous strategy of harmonizing with American accounting standards. The draft strategy recognizes that the Americans are now emphasizing an objectives-based approach; even so, our neighbours' standards are too rules-oriented to allow the kind of financial reporting that is seen as necessary to provide multiple stakeholders in Canada with the financial information they need.[22] Although Canadian standard setters are removing some of the discretion that managers once enjoyed when choosing accounting policies and applying accounting standards, they are retaining a "principles-based" approach.

## GAAP VERSUS (FIRST) PRINCIPLES: HOW SHOULD YOU APPROACH THESE CASES?

Your analyses of the cases in this book will vary with your background in accounting and the instructions of your professor. It is possible to analyze the cases without extensive knowledge of GAAP. In a first accounting course, for example, you will be introduced to the conceptual principles on which financial reporting is based. These first principles will be enough for you to understand the available alternatives in a given case; from this, you should be able to provide reasoned recommendations for how to proceed given those principles. At this point in your accounting education the focus is on the logic underlying the accounting model and on the ambiguities that emerge as you try to apply that model to specific circumstances.

---

[21] http://www.sec.gov/news/press/2003-86.htm.

[22] The ASBC strategy documents can be accessed through http://www.acsbcanada.org.

You may also use this book in courses later in your program when you begin to explore the details of GAAP or try to analyze financial statements for the purpose of making investment decisions. At this point in your understanding of accounting you will be able to recognize that some alternatives have been ruled out by current accounting standards. You may still believe that other options are better for specific stakeholders or for society as a whole than the financial disclosures mandated by standard setters. This is to be encouraged! Recall that GAAP is not fixed. It is a living consensus, and it changes over time as our understanding of the consequences of various reporting choices develops. Accounting standards are set by committees composed of the users and preparers of financial reports. These committees are subject to due-process requirements, which means that before a standard is implemented, input is sought from the people who will be affected. If you find yourself in disagreement with the standards, there are mechanisms for you to have your say; you can respond to exposure drafts of new standards, lobby to have standards reconsidered, or volunteer to sit on standard-setting committees.

Where GAAP does not constrain how financial statements are prepared, your analysis should start from first principles. Given the facts of the case and the objectives of the users of the financial statements, you should be able to identify the policies the company should prefer. Your recommendations may be consistent with GAAP, but they need not be if your analysis suggests that users would be better served by other approaches to accounting for the company's financial position and transactions.

Financial reporting, by its very nature, requires that judgment be exercised. The measurement and disclosure of the financial state of a company is not a matter of mechanically applying rules. Financial reporting is guided by the role that financial reports play in society and thus by the needs of the users of those reports. When faced with any set of business transactions, managers have choices to make about how those transactions should be measured, summarized, and reported. Users of financial statements when reading those reports must consider how the choices that have been made will affect how they interpret that information. The choices managers can make are constrained by accounting principles (GAAP) in some cases; even so, judgment is still required when principles are applied in particular circumstances. In addition, many businesses are not required to follow GAAP and may develop accounting policies that best meet their particular needs. To properly play their roles in this process, financial report preparers, auditors, and users need to develop judgment skills.

CHAPTER 3

# A GUIDE TO CASE ANALYSIS

Most students find case analysis frustrating and difficult. It is frustrating because a case does not provide prepackaged information that neatly fits the requirements of the analytical tools of accounting. A case will include the information that is essential to consider in coming to a recommendation, but it may also include information that is tangential or even misleading. Sometimes the information you need is not included in the case but is implied by the circumstances. For example, the industry in which a firm operates provides important clues about the business environment and the constraints under which financial reporting occurs. One of the important skills to develop is the ability to identify the information and assumptions that are crucial to your analysis.

Students find case analysis difficult because there is no one correct answer. Case analysis is not about applying fixed techniques to arrive at a number or other single solution. The lack of a correct answer, however, does not mean there are not better and worse answers. In part the quality of a case analysis is related to the process you follow and how you communicate this process. A good case analysis will provide evidence that you have applied sound diagnostic skills to the correct information, considered a reasonable set of alternatives, and made a reasoned recommendation. Two people may analyze the same case and come to completely opposite recommendations, yet each could be recognized as having done good work. The purpose of this brief guide is to help you understand the case analysis process and to write better case analyses.

There are many guides to case analysis to which you can refer. Figure 3.1 provides two alternatives to which you can compare the approach described below. Each of these approaches tends to cover the same ground and will help you develop a sound analysis. Like case analysis itself, the use of any guide to case analysis requires practice and good judgment. *Do not apply the guide in a mechanical or checklist manner. Think about what each step is asking you to do and why. Each step contributes towards making a reasoned recommendation based on consideration of a range of alternatives.*

**FIGURE 3.1:** Examples of Alternative Approaches to Case Analysis

From C.C. Lundberg and C. Enz (1993), "A Framework for Student Case Preparation," *Case Research Journal* 13 (Summer), p. 144.

- Step 1: Gaining Familiarity
  - a. In general — determine who, what, how, where and when (the critical facts in a case).
  - b. In detail — identify the places, persons, activities, and contexts of the situation.
  - c. Recognize the degree of certainty/uncertainty of acquired information.

- Step 2: Recognizing Symptoms
  - a. List all indicators (including stated "problems") that something is not as expected or as desired.
  - b. Ensure that symptoms are not assumed to be the problem (symptoms should lead to identification of the problem).

- Step 3: Identifying Goals
  - a. Identify critical statements by major parties (e.g., people, groups, the work unit, etc.).
  - b. List all goals of the major parties that exist or can be reasonably inferred.

- Step 4: Conducting the Analysis
  - a. Decide which ideas, models, and theories seem useful.
  - b. Apply these conceptual tools to the situation.
  - c. As new information is revealed, cycle back to sub-steps a and b.

- Step 5: Making the Diagnosis
  - a. Identify predicaments (goal inconsistencies).
  - b. Identify problems (discrepancies between goals and performance).
  - c. Prioritize predicaments/problems regarding timing, importance, etc.

- Step 6: Doing the Action Planning
  - a. Specify and prioritize the criteria used to choose action alternatives.
  - b. Discover or invent feasible action alternatives.
  - c. Examine the probable consequences of action alternatives.
  - d. Select a course of action.
  - e. Design an implementation plan/schedule.
  - f. Create a plan for assessing the action to be implemented.

From Richard Stillman (ed.), *Public Administration: Concepts and Cases,* 8th edition, Boston: Houghton Mifflin, 2005.

- Become familiar with case substance – facts, info, availability
- Determine central issues – decisions to be made, who is responsible, what are issues
- Identify objectives and goals to be achieved – what is possible, desirable
- Ascertain resources and constraints – what resources are available, what are obstacles, who supports and opposes

**FIGURE 3.1:** Examples of Alternative Approaches to Case Analysis (*Continued*)

- Ascertain the nature of the conflict – what is the substance of the conflict, can the issues be resolved
- Identify dynamics of behavior – who is leading, are there interpersonal conflicts, are stakeholders making effective arguments
- Determine major alternatives – what hasn't been considered, are alternatives complementary or mutually exclusive
- Assess consequences of likely decisions and actions – what actions are likely to result from decisions made, what are the unintended consequences
- Consider appropriate strategies and priorities – what are the most effective ways of achieving and implementing objectives and decisions, and are there intermediate stages/steps

To help you think about case analysis, we have broken down the process into the following stages:

- information gathering;
- issue identification;
- issue prioritization;
- alternative generation;
- recommendation; *and*
- implementation issues.

The case analysis process is summarized in Figure 3.2. We will elaborate on each of these stages below.

## INFORMATION GATHERING

The first stage in any case analysis is straightforward: read the case. In fact, you may need to read the case several times. In the rest of this guide you will learn what to look for as you read. In brief, you are reading to understand your role in completing the case analysis and to identify the key facts, the issues, the users of the information and their objectives, and any factors that may limit the range of alternatives that can be considered. Rosen[1] summarized what to look for as you read a case as the following mantra: *facts, objectives, constraints.*

### UNDERSTAND YOUR ASSIGNMENT

One of the most important parts of the case to understand is the "required" assignment. Most case analyses specifically ask you to prepare your analysis from the perspective of a particular role communicating to a particular person using a particular

---

[1] L.S. Rosen, *Financial Accounting: A Canadian Casebook,* Toronto: Prentice-Hall, 1982.

**FIGURE 3.2:** The Case Analysis Process

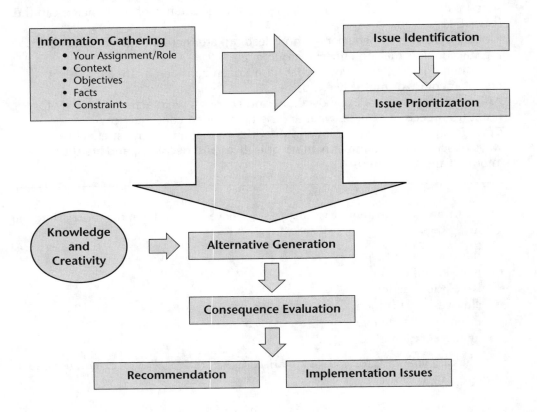

format. This is typically found in the final sentence or paragraph of the case. For example, you may be asked to assume the role of a staff accountant preparing a memo for the senior management of a public company, or you may be asked to provide a report to an audit partner from the perspective of an audit manager working on a private-company audit of financial statements to be submitted to a bank to support a loan application. The "required" part of the case is important because it provides the terms of reference for your assignment and, most importantly, for the "client" you are serving.

## UNDERSTAND THE CONTEXT

As part of your first reading of the case, identify any aspects of the business and its environment that may affect financial reporting. For example, identify the industry in which the company operates and any special regulations or laws that may apply. Determine whether the company is in good financial condition or in crisis. Identify who will use the financial reports and what decisions will be affected. Identify management's motives and incentives to make financial reporting choices in a particular way, and try to assess whether the information management is working with is reliable. (In large companies this may be a question of the quality of the internal control system — that is, the steps management has taken to ensure the reliability of the information on which it bases the financial statements; in smaller companies it may simply be a question of the competence of the manager making the key assumptions required by the financial reporting system.)

Discussing the case with others may help you identify important contextual factors. Based on our personal experiences, exposure to different businesses, and our own reading of the business press, each of us develops a store of tacit knowledge about how the world works. When you discuss cases in groups, you become aware that you have tacit knowledge that you can use to educate your peers and enrich your own analyses of cases. Don't be afraid to use this knowledge in your analyses; however, you may want to verify that what you "know" is valid. As we will discuss in the final chapter of this book, your understanding of the context of business will also improve as you take more courses in your program. You may not be able to identify all of the important contextual variables initially, but with practice your skill at this will improve.

## IDENTIFY *IMPORTANT* CASE FACTS

Too often, students when analyzing a case waste their time (and the time of the person reading the analysis) by repeating the facts of the case. Your analysis need only mention those facts which are relevant. Imagine that you and a friend are crossing a road and your friend is about to step off the curb in front of a car. What do you call out? Most likely you yell something short and forceful that will trigger the response that will save your friend's life, like "*Car!*" You probably don't yell: "Look! A black two-door late model sedan!" The key fact in this situation is the existence of the car because of the danger it poses to your friend's life. If on the other hand you and your friend were on a car dealer's lot looking for a particular type of car to buy, calling out the colour and style of the car would be relevant to the decision being made.

Any time case facts are mentioned in your case write-up they should move your analysis forward. The important facts are the ones that help you identify issues and evaluate alternatives. Do not just repeat case facts in your analysis — tell the reader why those facts are important to your analysis. If you have restated a case fact, ask yourself: "Why is this piece of information important to me? How does it affect my thinking about financial reporting for this company?" The most effective way to identify which case facts are important is to have a model or framework to guide your analysis.

Part of your instructor's role is to provide you with these frameworks, which you will practise using by applying them to the cases in this book. These frameworks may include tools for quantitative analysis. For example, the case might concern short-term cash flow problems. One way to identify such issues is to calculate financial statement ratios such as the quick ratio [(Current assets − Inventory)/Current liabilities]. The purpose of such frameworks is to help you identify — and in some cases create through calculations — the key data on which to base your analysis.

# ISSUE IDENTIFICATION

Most cases focus on a particular issue or set of issues. When reading the case keep a list of all of the issues you come across. In a financial reporting context, issues are any choices management must make regarding how to recognize, measure, or disclose transactions. Those choices will have a material impact on the welfare of any stakeholder.

It is important to use your own judgment when reading the issues identified by the characters in the case. It is not uncommon for people engulfed in problems to be unable to see the key issues clearly; your role is to provide an objective overview of the case.

# ISSUE PRIORITIZATION

You will probably encounter multiple issues in the case. Not all issues are equally important. It may not be crucial for you to spend a lot of time on some of the issues. The key is to prioritize them — that is, list them in order of importance. The importance of various issues depends on the objectives of the decision maker in the case and the consequences of the issues. Obviously, any issue that could affect the survival of the firm is central. An issue that is short-term and is likely to resolve itself is probably not worth acting on.

Be careful also to differentiate between symptoms and root causes. To diagnose issues successfully, you must be able to look beyond the symptoms to see what is causing the problem. For example, a company may be experiencing cash shortages and high turnover. A consultant who suggests a bank loan and employee recognition awards, but who misses the company's too rapid expansion and overworked key personnel, will not be helping the firm survive. The case may suggest that a key issue is how to disclose some transaction, but on analysis you may conclude that the company has not measured the transaction correctly, or you may conclude that the transaction has been not been recognized properly. Before trying to provide a solution, be sure you understand the issue.

# ALTERNATIVE GENERATION

Once the issues have been identified you must develop a plan of action. There will be multiple ways of handling each issue. You should be able to identify the key characteristics of each alternative — for example, how difficult or costly it would be to implement, how many of the issues in the case it would address, and what conflicts it might generate. Be sensitive to alternatives that are mutually exclusive or mutually supportive. Some steps would have to be taken at the same time in order for both to succeed; sometimes the opposite — taking two steps at the same time would negate both.

This is the part of case analysis where you can apply your creativity and knowledge. Your knowledge provides you with a set of possible responses; your creativity helps you recognize new applications for existing responses, potential variations on standard responses that would best fit the situation, and novel ways of addressing issues. One of the most serious blunders a case analyst can make is to jump immediately to a recommendation as "obvious" or "the only course of action possible" without exercising some creativity first. This is sometimes referred to as "ready, shoot, aim." You want to slow down before you pull the trigger and make sure you have the correct target in your sights. Be careful, too, not to create "straw men" among your alternatives. Straw men in this context are alternatives developed for the sole purpose of rejecting them. A person reading your analysis should be able to see that the alternatives you have considered are reasonable and reasonably comprehensive. If your alternatives are not well thought out, why should we believe your recommendation is?

## EVALUATE CONSEQUENCES

Once you have a list of alternatives, you must narrow the list down to one recommendation. To do this you must compare the consequences of each alternative and determine which one best meets the objectives of the decision maker. It is important at this point to consider both quantitative and qualitative outcomes. For example, strategic considerations sometimes require that the alternative with the best short-term financial outcome be rejected. It may be helpful at this stage to develop a set of criteria, based on the decision maker's objectives, to use in evaluating each alternative.

At this stage you may find there is no clear winner among your alternatives. Each of the alternatives may address a subset of the issues or have different cost/benefit tradeoffs. You may need to return to your earlier analysis and refine your identification of the objectives of your assignment or of the importance of various issues to ensure that you can identify the best alternative. You may also need to rethink your alternatives and ensure that you have been creative in considering what could be done. This is where "thinking outside the box" becomes valuable.

## RECOMMENDATION

Once you have decided on the best alternative, you must present your recommendation to the decision maker. Your recommendation must be fully justified in terms of that person's objectives and capabilities. For example, if the company is a family business and the problem in the case is the incompetence of the controller (who is also the president's nephew), your recommendation must be sensitive to this detail. Your recommendation should make a convincing case for implementation based on the analysis you have performed. This is not the time to add additional reasons or details! The recommendation is a summary of your analysis, not another step in the analysis. If you find that you must introduce new material to justify your recommendation, you probably need to go back to your analysis and make sure you have done a thorough job.

## IMPLEMENTATION ISSUES

Finally, you should consider how your recommendation will be implemented. In part you will have considered this issue in deciding which alternative to recommend, but depending on the case requirements, you may need to specify what will need to be done to implement your recommendation. This may involve, for example, indicating the order in which your recommendations should be implemented or what additional work — such as consultation with various parties or changes in operations — may be necessary to ensure success.

## GROUP CASE ANALYSIS

It is very common to have students do case analyses in groups or teams. This approach to case analysis provides you with practice with the problem-solving approach that is typically used in business — cross-functional teams are brought together to deal with key problems. When a team functions effectively, it generates better alternatives and makes better recommendations than an individual. When a team does not function effectively, it can be a frustrating and emotionally draining experience. Here are some guidelines for helping your team to produce an excellent case report:

1. *Be prepared.* Every member of the group must have done his/her reading and come to the group meeting prepared to participate.
2. *Take responsibility.* To use legal language, every member of the group is "joint and severally liable" for the outcome. In other words, every individual is responsible for the entire project. This has implications that are spelled out below. The group must establish very early what it expects of its members. If problems arise, they should be discussed and resolved within the group (this means moving the group to a higher level of functioning, not sweeping problems under the rug or reducing the team to a series of individual tasks).
3. *Challenge one another.* Although it may be convenient to assign tasks to different members of the group, *you* are responsible for the quality of the work done. All members must be willing to challenge one another (a) to ensure that each understands all the work that was done by the others, and (b) to be satisfied that the work meets everyone's standards of excellence. The final product must be a seamless report, not simply a merged set of individual documents. As a member of the team, you should be prepared to answer questions about any aspect of the final report, regardless of your specific contributions.
4. *Practise active listening.* To work effectively together, the team members must practise active listening skills. This means being open to other's opinions and respectful of differences; it also involves all the individual members providing feedback to demonstrate that they understand other members' positions and that everyone has been heard. When giving feedback, be specific and provide examples, and do so in a mutually supportive way, without being competitive or aggressive.

Group work is intended to improve the quality of case reports and the quality of the learning experience. It does so by exposing students to other perspectives and by encouraging them to develop key skills (such as leadership and follower skills, communication and negotiation skills, and organizational skills). Group work may not be the most efficient way to complete a task. It is used when the objective is to improve the quality of the work, not to get it done in the least amount of time. If your instructor has assigned a group case analysis, his/her expectations for the quality of the work will be higher than had the analysis been done by individuals. Keep this in mind!

## WRITING A CASE ANALYSIS

The format of your case analysis will be specified in the "required" section of the case assignment. It may be a short memo that highlights the essential aspects of your analysis, a letter to communicate your findings to clients, or a comprehensive report that will be used to brief others who are responsible for making a decision based on your recommendation. Regardless of the format, your case write-up should be concise, well organized, logical, and persuasive.[2]

### MEMO

A memo, or memorandum, is used to communicate between people in the same organization. This form of communication is typically less formal and shorter than a letter or report. A memo is concise, coherent, and sharply focused. It should include a brief introduction to frame the subject of the memo, a paragraph or paragraphs providing the body of the message, and, where appropriate, a brief conclusion. The conclusion may offer further help or contact information or simply a courteous goodbye.

### LETTER

A letter is memo directed to people *outside* the organization. Since it is addressed to clients or written on behalf of clients, its tone tends to be more formal. Since it may be addressed to someone without technical knowledge of the subject, great care must be taken to avoid jargon and to ensure that the meaning is unambiguous.

### REPORT

Reports are used to communicate a comprehensive analysis of a case. Typically a report will include a letter (or memo) of transmittal that alerts the reader to the purpose of the report and its main conclusions or recommendations. A report's structure

---

[2] For a more comprehensive guide see C. May and G.S. May, *Effective Writing: A Handbook for Accountants*, 4th edition, Upper Saddle River, NJ: Prentice Hall, 1996.

depends on its length and complexity, but a fairly long report typically contains a contents list, an executive summary, and an introduction, body, and conclusions. As appropriate, the report may include appendices (typically for illustrative data or detailed calculations that would reduce the body text's readability if it were included there), a bibliography, and any figures or graphics to which the body text refers. The body of the report should provide enough detail that the reader can understand the logic and analysis that supports the development of alternatives and its recommendations or conclusions.

## WHAT TO LOOK FOR IN A GOOD CASE ANALYSIS

Before leaving this chapter we want to stress once more that this guide to case analysis is not a checklist to be applied mechanically. Simply having headings that cover all the items discussed above and presenting your analysis in the format specified in the "required" section of the case will not make it a good case analysis. This guide reflects a set of principles about case analysis. A good case analysis is sensitive to the facts of the case; it interprets those facts using sound knowledge, identifies and prioritizes the issues facing the decision maker, creatively constructs and justifies alternatives, provides a recommendation based on a careful assessment of the costs and benefits of each alternative, and provides guidance for implementing the recommendation. A good case write-up provides evidence of the analysis process that you followed and is written clearly and persuasively.

Doing a good case analysis — in fact, doing a sound analysis of any business decision — is not easy! It requires a set of skills, which must be honed by practice and exercised with diligence and creativity. You will be able to develop these skills by using this book.

# C H A P T E R 4

# AN EXAMPLE CASE ANALYSIS

This chapter provides you with a sample case analysis. The case is presented in the same format as other cases in the book. It is followed by a response to the case written by the case author in the format a student would be expected to submit for an assignment or exam answer. You may want to read the case and prepare your own response before reading the instructor's "solution." Remember that legitimate differences of opinion do arise in the analysis of cases and in the construction of alternatives and recommendations; the "solution" provided here is not the only correct answer to the case. Pay particular attention to the way in which the case write-up identifies and discusses alternatives. This is a key aspect of the critical thinking skills you will develop while analyzing cases.

This chapter should be read in conjunction with Chapter 5. The case presented in Chapter 5 is slightly more complex than the one presented here; of particular note are differences in the format of the case solution. Again we emphasize that a case analysis must be tailored to fit its circumstances. In this chapter the assignment is to prepare an e-mail response to a set of issues raised by your boss. In the next chapter the assignment is to prepare a report for an unsophisticated client. Compare these two case analyses, looking for similarities in the process the author followed (identifying and prioritizing issues, generating alternatives, evaluating the consequences of the alternatives, making a recommendation, and where necessary pointing out implementation issues). Also look for differences between the case solutions and consider why the author decided to be more formal in the report provided in Chapter 5 than in the e-mail provided in Chapter 4. Why are the alternatives set out explicitly in Chapter 5, and why is there less discussion of alternatives in Chapter 4?

If you treat the case *solutions* in Chapters 4 and 5 as cases to be analyzed, you will learn more about the process of case analysis than you would just from reading these as "solutions." In other words, study the solutions to understand the process of case analysis; do not simply read them as responses to particular cases. To facilitate your understanding of the process of case analysis and write-up, we have annotated the solution with footnotes describing the essential aspects of the analysis and the key choices that were made. As you will see in these footnotes, the model of case analysis presented in Chapter 3 was modified to fit the specifics of this case: some steps were omitted or required very little work, whereas other steps are shown in detail. This reinforces the point made in Chapter 3: *Don't apply the guide in a mechanical or checklist manner. Think about what each step is asking you to do and why. Each step contributes towards making a reasoned recommendation based on consideration of a range of alternatives.*

While the guidelines will help ensure that you have not missed anything in your case analysis, you must use the guidelines as principles to be modified to fit the nature of the case and the requirements of the analysis and write-up.

# LEDD

## *Kevin Markle*

You are employed as a junior accounting advisor at the accounting firm of Fun, Wow, & How, LLP. You were sitting at your desk today pretending to work when an e-mail arrived from your boss, Beka Huna. Ms. Huna is currently in Calgary at the headquarters of Ledd Inc., a client of the firm that manufactures and sells computers. The following is the e-mail from Ms. Huna:

Hello,

I am currently on lunch break from a meeting with the CFO and accounting department here at Ledd. There are some pretty big decisions that need to be made before this year's (fiscal year ended October 31, 2004) financial statements are ready to be audited. They have already put the auditor off twice, so we have to get these decisions made quickly. And the bank has been asking for statements for a month. I am fairly sure I know what recommendations to make on the issues, but I wanted to check with you to be sure I have not missed some angles in my thinking. I'm asking you because I know you have a solid understanding of the issues at hand.

I need you to prepare a brief but thorough memo for me. I will only have about an hour to review it over the dinner hour. We have all agreed to work tonight to reach conclusions. As such, I need your memo to be e-mailed back to me within the next two hours, preferably one. I realize this is short notice, but please don't cut corners because you are rushing. If we give bad advice here, we could be sued. Remember . . . I won't be able to ask you any questions, so be sure to make it clear in your memo the reasoning behind your recommendations.

Here are the basics of what is going on:

1. The loan from the bank has a covenant attached stating that if the debt-to-equity ratio exceeds 1.5:1, the bank can call the loan. If the loan were to be called, Ledd would be crippled. At this point, Ledd is on-side, but there is not much room for comfort.

2. Ledd has an extensive profit-sharing plan whereby management receives a bonus based on the net income reported on the financial statements.

3. Ledd made a very large purchase of new automated equipment in August 2004. The equipment cost $4,000,000 and is expected to last for 5 years. There was a delay in getting the equipment operational because the installation (which cost an additional $300,000) could not be done until October 27, 2004. No amortization expense has been recorded for the equipment for fiscal 2004, and they have recorded the installation cost as part of the cost of the asset.

4. Inventory is a big problem. They have always used FIFO to value the year-end inventory and arrive at the cost-of-goods-sold figure. However, the pace of technology change continues to increase, so they are consistently purchasing newer (and more expensive) versions of parts before they have used up the ones in stock. I have a feeling the inventory could be overvalued by as much as $1.5M. They contend that as long as they are consistent with their policy, everything is fine.

5. Ledd has done a fantastic job of reducing the turn-around time between customer order and shipping of the product (it is now an average of 6 business days). As such, they have modified their accounting system to record the revenue from a sale at the time of order rather than at the time of shipping. I checked prior years, and there would be no material difference in the financial statements of prior years if the policy were applied retroactively. However, they did receive a very large order ($1M+) from a corporate customer on October 27, 2004.

6. Ledd began selling to some overseas markets this year and landed some big contracts, for which they have booked substantial revenues. The collection of these amounts (they have made all the sales on credit) has been really slow. They haven't booked any bad debt expense because they are brand-new in these markets and don't have a basis on which to make the estimate.

These are the main issues. Please send me your memo as soon as possible.

Many thanks,

Beka Huna

## Required

Draft the memo for Ms. Huna.

# LEDD – SUGGESTED SOLUTION[1]

## *Kevin Markle*

To:     Beka Huna

From:   Junior Accountant

Re:     Ledd's October 31, 2004, financial statements[2]

## Context

From what you have described, there are three users of note: the shareholders, the bank, and management.[3] While a general stewardship objective is overriding, the client needs accounting that will keep the debt-to-equity ratio on-side and that will be acceptable to the auditor. An approach focusing on maintaining the debt-to-equity ratio should be acceptable to management since it will likely lead to higher bonuses earlier.[4] GAAP is a constraint on the alternatives that would be acceptable, and the auditor will be verifying compliance. Scrutiny will be high because of the debt covenant and the fact that the auditor has been delayed twice.[5] Your message is clear that overly aggressive policies should not be recommended due to the sensitive conditions. Time is also a constraint on the recommendations we make because the short time window may make it infeasible to implement some changes in the current year.

---

[1] This "solution" is one of many possible ways of responding to the requirements of the case. When reading this section, focus on the process of analysis that underlies the write-up. Feel free to recommend alternative solutions based on your own analysis.

[2] The "information gathering" for this case can be done very quickly since the case is very directive (i.e., she states overtly what she wants you to do and how she wants you to do it). Because of the unique circumstances in the case, repetition of the facts to her would definitely be wasted time, since you would be telling her what she has just told you.

[3] There is no need to explain the relevance of the users (i.e., why you are considering them) in this case because the reader is a superior who is assumed to have this knowledge. In other cases with different clients, such an explanation would be necessary.

[4] This sentence integrates two important case facts — the covenant and management's inherent bias.

[5] This sentence integrates two important case facts — the statements will be audited, and they are already late.

I have done my best to be as specific as possible, but there are some issues that cannot be fully resolved based on the information I have. I have identified those issues for you.[6]

## Capital Assets[7]

There are a number of issues here. I have identified and will discuss them separately.

*Installation cost* — Capitalizing it is beneficial for the ratio and will not be challenged by the auditor because it is a cost necessary to ready the asset for use.[8] If allocations of staff time or existing resources are in the $300,000 range, we will need to ensure that the basis of allocation is reasonable.

*Amortization* — Taking no amortization is clearly desirable for its effect on the ratio. A full year would be $800,000 (assuming straight-line), 3 months would be $200,000.[9] There is a reasonable basis for recording no amortization on the assumption that their amortization policy is based on usage rather than the simple passage of time. This is a reasonable assumption for manufacturing equipment, but should be confirmed.

---

[6] The "issue identification" in this case is not very difficult since the information is presented in a list and is very concise. However, students should be very wary of approaching cases under the assumption that "1 list item = 1 issue." There are often multiple issues arising from the information in one item (e.g., item 3 in this case). And there are often list items that do not contain issues at all, but instead provide facts or information relevant to the context (e.g., items 1 and 2 in the above list). An important step in preparing an outline is making your own list of the issues. Relying on an itemized list can easily result in missed issues and/or wasted time.

[7] "Issue prioritization" is not an important step in this particular case since there are not very many issues to be dealt with and all of them are important to the "client" (your boss). This solution addresses the issues in the order they are given in the case since there is not an obvious basis on which to prioritize them. If one wanted to prioritize in a case like this, the most reasonable basis would be the size of the impact on the ratio. The inventory issue would rank above the capital asset issue. However, we are not able to quantify the impact of the other two issues.

[8] A student following a "template" approach would likely identify and discuss the alternative of these costs being expensed in the current year. There may be cases in which such a discussion would provide value to the client, but here there is clearly no need to discuss the alternatives.

[9] Students may perceive an inconsistency between this and the discussion in note 2 above in that we are really telling the reader something she already knows. While it is true that she could just as easily derive these numbers on her calculator, they are included because they help quantify the issue before we get to our recommendation. Decisions on inclusion or exclusion of information are not easily made because there is often reasonable justification for both. Such decisions should always be made based on whether they provide value to the client. We often make statements of facts of which the client is already aware, but we make them so that they anchor the thoughts which follow.

The issue of the 4 days of operation is likely under the auditor's materiality level (even though it is likely very low in these circumstances). However, it is reasonable that no amortization would be recorded because it is very unlikely that 4 days of operation contributed to revenue that is to be recognized this year.

*Tax* — An additional consideration is the accounting for taxes. The asset will be amortized for tax (i.e., capital cost allowance will be taken on the tax return — the half-year rule likely applies) because it was put into operation in the year. Assuming they use future-income-tax reporting, this will create a temporary difference that will create a future tax liability and increase the tax expense for the year (and harm the ratio).[10] This is unavoidable under GAAP unless differential reporting is an option.[11] I don't know what the shareholder profile of the company is, but if it is possible to obtain unanimous shareholder consent, they could use differential reporting and opt to use the taxes-payable method. However, due to the time constraint, it is unlikely that a change could be made for this year.

## Inventory

It appears that they have not been using an appropriate cost-flow assumption. Is the full $1.5M in excess value a result of this year? Not knowing the size of the total inventory, I find this hard to believe. Did the auditor miss this in previous years?

Based on what you have told me, LIFO or average cost would be more appropriate on an ongoing basis, but that is really not relevant this year. A change to LIFO or average cost would require a retroactive restatement. Depending on the complexities involved, this may not be possible to complete in the time we have. In addition, since LIFO is not permitted for tax purposes, adopting it would require the tracking of costs under two cost-flow methods (one for accounting, one for tax). This may be prohibitively

---

[10] This is a good example of an issue that is "hidden." There is nothing in the given facts that leads us to this issue, but it is an important issue that requires resolution.

[11] Depending on when this case is used, this may be an issue that students are not expected to identify because they have not been taught either future tax reporting or differential reporting. It should be kept in mind for all cases that student responses will be expected to be consistent with their progress in learning the various topics in financial accounting.

costly and complicated when compared to the benefit gained in financial statement usefulness.[12] The bottom line is that the inventory must be reported at the lower of cost and market. The auditor will not accept a treatment that does not result in inventory being reported at lower of cost and market. FIFO is an acceptable cost-flow method as long as year-end valuations are completed and any necessary write-downs are made.

The determination of the value as at October 31, 2004, will be somewhat problematic since time has passed. However, I assume that a count was done and attended by the auditor. It is imperative that an accurate value be determined. To write it down based on an estimate would not be advisable as there is significant impact on the ratio. I understand that the time constraint will be problematic, but steps towards obtaining an independent valuation should be taken.

**Revenue Recognition**

This change will be challenged by the auditor, so our justification needs to be solid. First and foremost, if the additional revenue is to be recognized this year, the products' costs must also be accrued this year for the purposes of matching.[13] This could be done easily as it is assumed that they have fairly consistent gross margins on their products. To have revenue with no cost of goods sold would be unreasonable.

Can we justify the early revenue recognition? There is no question that it is aggressive. The auditor will question the basis on which they are considering it earned at the point of order. Because it is a physical product, the risks and rewards would seem to transfer with ownership (assumed to be established by possession). Their only basis for supporting the change would be a solid history showing very minimal cancellations

---

[12] The preceding sentences of this paragraph are not very useful to the reader of the report, and an argument could be made for excluding them entirely. They are included in this solution on the assumption that Ms. Huna is contemplating a change of cost-flow method. This is an example of an issue on which a student using a "template" approach would waste significant time. Such a student would likely identify the alternatives of the three methods, discuss the advantages and disadvantages of each, and conclude that FIFO is the best one for the client based on objectives. But that provides no value to the client in this case because the issue is the valuation, not the cost-flow method.

[13] This is often overlooked by students when considering "revenue recognition" issues; they will often conclude that it is okay to record revenue ahead of shipment without considering that that may result in revenue and the direct costs of that revenue being reported in different years.

between point of order and shipment. We can leave it as it is and see what the auditor does with it. There is enough to support the early recognition as plausible, so there is no risk of us giving advice that leads to intentional misstatement.[14] The client has to understand that this brings actual gross margin from next year into this year. If similar sales do not happen next year, this helps the ratio in the short term, but will have no impact in the long run if actual sales do not continue to occur.

**Bad Debts**

It is very unlikely that the auditor will accept no bad debt expense for the sales in the new markets. The only way this would be acceptable is if the client has some evidence that bad debts are known to be less frequent in those markets than in the Canadian market. It is doubtful that this is the case.

There are likely sources of information on the markets available from research firms or consulting companies. If these options have been explored and have not yielded reliable information, a baseline would be to apply the method and rates used for determining the amount for the sales in the Canadian market. This may be advantageous in the short term if actual collection problems in the new markets turn out to be worse than in the Canadian market because it will defer the reduction of equity to a future period.[15]

These are the recommendations I have for you. I'm sorry I could not be more concrete, but it is difficult to be specific without knowing the full fact situation. I hope I have provided what you were looking for.

---

[14] As we often do in both real life and in cases, we are walking a thin line on ethics in a situation like this. It is very important to recognize that we are not helping our client to cheat or break the rules; if we do that, we put ourselves clearly on the wrong side of the ethics line. This issue comes down to whether the revenue can be considered "earned" prior to shipment of the goods. The reality is that in the real world, revenue is sometimes justifiably recorded in such situations. Another reality is that revenue is sometimes unjustifiably recorded by unethical people in such situations. Students will deal with many such situations and will come to appreciate the importance of ethics in accounting decision making.

[15] This is another time in which the explanations are very shallow because of the assumed sophistication of the reader. For a less sophisticated reader, it would be necessary to explain the alternatives (making no accrual for bad debts, accruing based on the Canadian market, or "guessing" at the bad debts for the new market) and the effects of each on the ratio. That is not necessary or valuable for this reader, so is not included.

# CHAPTER 5

# A SECOND EXAMPLE CASE ANALYSIS

This is the second sample case analysis. This chapter should be read in conjunction with Chapter 4 since there are differences in how the solutions to the two cases are approached. You will learn more about how to write up your case analyses if you take the time to identify the differences and similarities between the two solutions. You should find that the process of case analysis is the same in each chapter (identifying and prioritizing issues, generating alternatives, evaluating the consequences of the alternatives, making a recommendation, and where necessary pointing out implementation issues) but that the format of the write-up varies to meet the "required" part of the case.

To facilitate your understanding of the process of case analysis and write-up, we have annotated the solution with footnotes describing the essential aspects of the analysis and the key choices that were made. As you will see in these footnotes, the model of case analysis presented in Chapter 3 was modified to fit the specifics of this case: some steps were omitted or required very little work; other steps are shown in detail. This reinforces the point made in Chapter 3: *Do not apply the guide in a mechanical or checklist manner. Think about what each step is asking you to do and why. Each step contributes towards making a reasoned recommendation based on consideration of a range of alternatives.*

While the guidelines will help make sure you haven't missed anything in your case analysis, you must use the guidelines as principles to be modified to fit the nature of the case and the requirements of the analysis and write-up.

This case is slightly more complex than the one in Chapter 4. The write-up uses a format that is different from the one in Chapter 4 in that it provides an explicit list of alternatives followed by a discussion and recommendation. This format is appropriate given that the assignment is to provide a report to a client (manager), who must make her own decision about what form the accounting should take. As you read the case and its "solution," do not just accept this as the only way to complete the case requirement. How would *you* have responded to the case requirement? Are there elements of the "solution" you disagree with? Would you have presented the solution in a different way? The critical thinking process you are developing in this book starts now!

# HANNAH CONFECTIONS

## *Kevin Markle*

Robyn Hannah started Hannah Confections Inc. (Hannah) in early 2003. Her goal was to build the company gradually while she continued to work full-time at her job in research and development at a pharmaceutical company and then eventually quit her job and run Hannah. She invested $20,000 of her own money in exchange for the 100 common shares issued in 2003, and the company purchased some equipment and rented some warehouse space with the money. Soon after those initial transactions, Robyn found that she did not have enough time to get Hannah going while working full-time. In June 2004 she decided to take the leap. She quit her job and is now spending all her time on Hannah.

Hannah is a candy company. Robyn believes it can do very well with a new type of candy that contains some essential vitamins. She has researched the market and is confident she has come up with an idea for two unique products for which there is no competition. The first thing Hannah had to do, of course, was develop the products and have them accepted by the regulators. To that end, the company secured financing from two sources. The first was a venture capital company called VenCap. VenCap made an investment of $800,000 in exchange for 200 newly issued common shares. VenCap agreed to allow Robyn to continue to manage the company, but set the condition that her compensation must be a lower-than-market salary with an annual bonus of 10% of the reported net income.

Hannah also obtained a loan of $1.5 million from a bank. The loan was specifically intended to fund the purchase of equipment and was secured on that equipment (meaning that if Hannah did not make interest payments, the bank could take ownership of the equipment). A condition of the loan is that Hannah must pay to have a market value appraisal done on the equipment at the end of each fiscal year and provide that appraisal to the bank. As long as Hannah makes annual interest payments, the bank will use the annual appraisal as its sole source of information in making decisions related to the loan.

The first product, a chewable candy that Robyn had worked on over the past eighteen months, has already been approved by the regulators. Hannah has now begun marketing it and has some customers. She has shipped large quantities of the product to retailers across the country and has included invoices with all the shipments. The invoices require the customer to pay the full balance within sixty days of receipt of goods. As of today, October 8, 2004, she has received payment on fewer than 30% of the shipments made since the product was launched in June. More than 75% of all the shipments made since June were made in the past four weeks to take advantage of the peak Halloween season.

Because it is a new product, Robyn has given the customers one month from date of receipt to return the goods for a full refund if they are unsatisfied with them. So far no customer has returned goods.

The second product, a lollipop with an edible stick, is currently being developed in the Hannah labs. Robyn is very hopeful that the product will be finished and approved in time for the upcoming Christmas season.

Hannah used the bank loan to purchase some customized equipment for making the two types of candy. Robyn does not know how long the machines will last or how much product they will produce. The equipment that was purchased in early 2003 is mostly obsolete now, and Robyn is trying to sell it.

Robyn has chosen a December 31 year end for Hannah. She had never done any accounting for the company while it was inactive, but now she realizes she must prepare some financial statements. To this end she has come to you, an accounting advisor, for help. She has asked you to prepare a report for her that includes recommendations for how things should be accounted for. She will use your report as the basis for her instructions to the bookkeeper she plans to hire soon.

## Required

Prepare the report for Robyn Hannah.

## HANNAH CONFECTIONS — SUGGESTED SOLUTION[1]

*Kevin Markle*

To:     Robyn Hannah

From:   Accounting advisor

Re:     Financial statements of Hannah Confections Inc.

Before we can proceed to discussing the treatment of specific issues, we need to determine a context for the recommendations that will be made. Hannah is not a public company, so it may be possible to prepare financial statements outside of the constraints of GAAP. Financial statements are essentially a communication tool, and GAAP offers a set of rules and principles that constrain what is reported on financial statements when they are intended for public distribution. However, it may be possible to prepare more useful statements outside of the confines of GAAP. To make this decision, we must consider the users of the statements.[2] From the information I have, there are three main

---

[1] This "solution" is one of many possible ways of responding to the requirements of the case. When reading this section, focus on the process of analysis that underlies the write-up. Feel free to recommend alternative solutions based on your own analysis.

[2] As we read the case and gather information, it is crucial that we understand who the client is and what she wants from us (review "Understand the context" in Chapter 3). In this case, the client is not sophisticated in her understanding of accounting, so it will be necessary to explain things in simple terms and avoid jargon.

users of the financial statements of Hannah: VenCap, the bank, and you.[3] Each approaches the statements with different needs and objectives. VenCap is going to use them to evaluate the performance of the company as a whole and of you as its manager. The bank is a secured creditor and has indicated that the financial statements will be of secondary importance to them.[4] You would like to see high net income reported since part of your compensation is in the form of a bonus. Because you have relinquished control of the company to VenCap in order to accomplish what you want to accomplish, it is of primary importance that the statements reflect the company's performance.

So I recommend that the statements not be constrained by GAAP. GAAP will serve as a starting point,[5] but it is not always effective at capturing an entity's performance. It is imperative that you confirm with VenCap and the bank that they will be willing to receive non-GAAP financial statements and that they will not require an audit. If either requires the statements to be GAAP-compliant, those statements will have to be prepared that way and I will have to alter some of the recommendations below. However, I will proceed on the assumption that all users are amenable to using non-GAAP statements.

Before proceeding to the issues I have identified, I want to suggest that you consider a different year end for the company.[6] A corporation is allowed to choose any day as the end of its fiscal year. Because of the seasonal nature of your business (with large quantities of sales in the Christmas season), a December 31 year end will result in

---

[3] Students who try to approach cases using a template or a checklist will often consider the users/uses/objectives as one of the first steps in doing a case. It is very important to remember that we are writing a report for the client. Walking through a checklist will be of limited value to the client if we don't also convey the relevance of what we are doing to her in language she can understand.

[4] This is a key case fact that could easily be overlooked by a student using a template approach. The bank has said it will rely most heavily on an annual market value appraisal. This does *not* mean the bank expects the assets to be reported on the financial statements at their market value. It means that their primary tool for evaluating the company is something separate from the financial statements (the appraisal), so their use of the financial statements is secondary.

[5] Many students struggle with what "non-GAAP" actually means. Almost all of the fundamental concepts and guidelines that are taught are from the *CICA Handbook* and therefore part of GAAP. So if the statements are not constrained by GAAP, what rules and guidelines are we using? Do we just make up whatever we want? Clearly, that will not be useful unless we can fully explain our brand-new methods to everyone who will ever use the financial statements for anything. Instead, when we are not constrained by GAAP, we use it as a starting point; however, we then choose a non-GAAP alternative if doing so allows us to convey better information to the users of the statements.

[6] This is not an accounting issue, but it is clearly an area in which we can provide value by bringing information to the client's attention. The avoidance of estimates in accruals and deferrals will go a long way towards making the annual financial statements a better tool for evaluating the performance of the company.

a lot of estimates being necessary for the accrual and deferral of revenues and expenses. If a year end in the summer was chosen, this would likely not be an issue. The company was started in 2003 and it is now October 2004, so it is likely that at least one set of financial statements will have to be prepared retroactively. (Thus if the company was incorporated on April 1, 2003, and you choose a July 31 year end, financial statements — and tax returns — will have to be prepared for April 1, 2003, to July 31, 2003, and for August 1, 2003, to July 31, 2004. This will not be difficult since the company had nominal activity until June 2004.)

## Chewable Candy[7]

There are a few issues surrounding this product.

## Costs of Development

I am assuming that the $20,000 you originally invested was used to develop the product. If any costs were paid by you personally, they should be reimbursed to you (either in cash or by loan) and added to the $20,000.[8] In addition, it is presumed that most of the work was done by you for no pay. If no amount is included for the work you did, the performance of the company will not be captured accurately. If VenCap agrees to it, retroactive compensation should be given to you (in cash or loan or shares) so that the amount is recorded.

The bigger question is whether the $20,000 (plus the other amounts determined) should be recorded as expenses or as an asset. That is, we must determine *when*

---

[7] The identification of issues is an important step in a case like this one because the issues are not bulleted or laid out for us. It would be very beneficial for the student to have an outline listing the issues and prioritizing them before beginning to write. This response tackles the issues in the order in which they appear in the question because the expectation is that all issues will be covered fully since there was no time constraint in preparing the response. In an exam situation the prioritization of the issues is important because it ensures that the most significant problems are given the most attention if the student starts to run out of time. In this case, revenue recognition and research and development are the most important issues to the client.

[8] This "issue" seems minor because of the dollar value given in the case, but it is a very important principle that we are providing to the client here. When she was running the business by herself and for herself, this was really not very important. But now that there are other significant users of the financial statements to be considered, it becomes much more crucial that all activities be captured. In almost all cases we are brought in at a point at which there has been a major change. Here the major change is the introduction of large equity and debt investors. Comparing the pre-change environment to the post-change environment often yields strong clues about where we can provide value to our client.

these expenditures should be recorded on the income statement: if we treated them as an expense in the current year, they would be included on this year's income statement; if we recorded them as an asset, we would report them on the balance sheet in the current year and record them as expenses in future years.[9]

*Alternative 1:* "Expense as incurred." GAAP treats all amounts incurred for research as expenses because there is little certainty of future benefit or the measurement thereof.

*Alternative 2:* "Treat the expenditures as an asset to be amortized (expensed) against the revenue they will help bring in." If you chose this alternative, it will be difficult to determine a life over which to amortize the expenditures.

*Recommendation:*[10] To capture the company's performance[11] on each income statement, alternative 2 is the better choice. Assuming that you incurred significant costs to research and develop the project, it would be best to have those costs reflected on the same income statements as the revenues they helped produce. Since the product has been approved and sold, there is sufficient evidence of future benefit to those costs. To determine an appropriate amortization period, we would need to look at any industry information you have to determine the expected life for such a product.

**Revenue Recognition**

Because product and cash are not changing hands at the same time, there is some uncertainty as to when the revenue generated by the sales should be recognized.

*Alternative 1:* "At point of shipment." At this point the revenue is earned and the costs are known. However, there is some uncertainty regarding both the measurement of the

---

[9] This explanation is necessary because of the client's sophistication level. If this were written to an experienced accountant, "capitalize versus expense" would be sufficient to convey the issue.

[10] We are an advisor to the client. We are not making the final decision — the client is. That is why it is crucial for the client to understand there are alternative treatments available and what the ramifications of those alternatives are. She has every right not to take your recommendation. Whether she does or she does not, you have provided more value by allowing her to fully understand each of the alternatives.

[11] To help the client understand that our recommendations are appropriate for her specific situation, it is important that we "close the loop" for her by tying our recommendations back to the objectives we identified at the beginning.

amount (due to returns) and the collection (since you have no payment history as all customers are new). If revenue is recognized at this point, allowances for returns and for bad debts will have to be estimated.

*Alternative 2:* "At end of return period." This would remove the need to estimate returns and would also reduce the lag between revenue recognition and cash collection. As customers have one month to return, delaying the revenue to this point would delay it by one month from alternative 1 and reduce the uncertainty in estimates of bad debts.

*Alternative 3:* "At cash collection."[12] This would drastically reduce the need for estimates since in most cases cash would be coming in after the return period had expired. This could defer the recognition of the revenue by sixty days or more from alternative 1.

*Recommendation:* In order to capture performance, we want to record revenues at the point at which the economic exchange occurs. The reality is that this occurs before the customer pays. Both alternative 1 and alternative 2 are reasonable. The only real advantage that alternative 2 provides is that it removes the need to estimate returns. This is not that large an advantage because annual financial statements will usually not be prepared within one month of year end. Therefore, accurate information will be available to make the "estimate" under alternative 1. As such, I recommend that you recognize revenue at the time of shipment. The estimates of bad debt expense and returns will have to be based on any information you can obtain from industry sources since you do not have your own history with any of these customers. This may result in imprecise estimates in the early going, but the differences should not be materially large. Once you have some history, you will be able to base your estimates on that.

## Lollipop

The same issues of revenue and cost recognition will pertain to this product when it starts to be sold. However, the treatment of costs being incurred now is a trickier issue.

---

[12] Some may see this alternative as a "straw man" (see Chapter 3) — that is, an alternative offered only to be rejected. It is included here on the assumption that it is the option the unsophisticated client might have chosen. As such, it is important to explain its deficiencies to the client.

## Research and Development

*Alternative 1:* "Capitalize the costs of research." This is what I recommended for the first product. However, that product already had approval and was being sold (and therefore had some assurance of generating revenue). All I know about this product is that you are hopeful about it. There is no assurance it will ever be approved and saleable.[13]

*Alternative 2:* "Expense the costs of research." When discussing the chewable candy, I mentioned that GAAP convention is to expense research costs as they are incurred. I am assuming that you are not constrained by GAAP; still, there must be a compelling reason to depart from it.

*Recommendation:* I recommend you use alternative 1 and treat the costs as an asset. This is similar to what I recommended for the chewable candy. It will be important to disclose and explain this treatment to the bank and VenCap. The bank will not want to lend against this "asset." I feel this is the best choice, in that it will yield financial statements that will be useful in evaluating performance because revenues and expenses will be on the same income statements. There is a drawback to this approach: "What will happen if the product fails to receive approval?" The answer: You will have a large asset sitting on the balance sheet that will have to be written off as a one-time charge to the income statement, and there will be no revenue to match it to. Again, if all users understand how it is being treated, this will not be that problematic. Alternative 1 is the better choice, because alternative 2 would result in all expenses being recorded first and then all revenues being recorded in future years when the product is approved and sold. This would not indicate the performance of the company in a given year and would not show growth and trends accurately.

---

[13] It is very important to convey to the client that although the two issues look the same and have the same alternatives, the circumstances surrounding them are different and therefore the issues must be analyzed separately. A template approach would make this issue look exactly like the similar decision on the chewable candy. We provide much more value to the client when we help her understand how the differences in circumstances may lead to differences in accounting.

## Customized Equipment

These costs will be capitalized (i.e., recorded as an asset and expensed in future periods). There is no reasonable alternative.[14]

The issue that has to be resolved is how to amortize the costs on the income statement (i.e., how to determine a reasonable method of depreciating the assets). You have told me you don't know how long the machines will last or how much they will produce. I am assuming you have consulted the equipment's manufacturer and other industry sources and found no reliable information.

*Alternative 1:* "Use the depreciation method prescribed by the Income Tax Act." The ITA specifies the method and rate for every asset a company owns (this is known as capital cost allowance [CCA]). Although the ITA is not most concerned with depreciating an asset over its useful life, this is a reliable basis for determining annual depreciation.

*Alternative 2:* "Use straight-line over the life of the product being produced." Because the equipment is customized, it may only be useful for producing the products you have in production currently. If that is so, it could be amortized over the same life you have estimated for the amortization of the research costs.

*Recommendation:* You are most concerned with producing statements that will allow users to evaluate the performance of the company, so I would recommend alternative 1. Although this would not be acceptable under GAAP, it is the better choice in your situation because alternative 2 requires large estimates for which there appear to be no basis. For the purposes of capturing performance, depreciation of capital assets just needs to provide some systematic allocation of the cost over the life of the asset. Either alternative will provide that, so I have recommended the more reliable one.[15]

---

[14] A student applying a template or checklist could waste significant time listing and analyzing the "capitalize and expense" "alternatives." That would provide no value to the client, so it is not done.

[15] There is an additional point that could be made here regarding future income taxes — that is, that using CCA rates prevents temporary differences and avoids the need for future income tax accounting. It is a judgment call whether such information would provide value to the client or not. It is not included in this response on the assumption that it would confuse the client and is not necessary because the recommendation not to follow GAAP was made at the beginning (thus the taxes-payable method would be used for accounting for taxes). A brief explanation of the issue (and why we are avoiding it in her case) in simple terms may have value for the client. Such decisions are left to the discretion of the individuals preparing and reading the report.

## Equipment Held for Sale[16]

It is assumed that these assets did not have significant costs since they were purchased with only a portion of the initial $20,000 (the rest going to rent and other
costs). Similar to what I said regarding the research of the chewable candy, if you
incurred costs personally for the purchase or upkeep of this equipment, those amounts
should be accounted for.

*Alternative 1:* "Record it as a capital asset until it is sold and then record a gain or a
loss." This alternative is simple and records nothing until actual transactions take
place.

*Alternative 2:* "Report the assets separately as 'assets held for sale' and write them
down to their market value." This is what GAAP prescribes for such situations. It
results in the income statement impact from a loss happening before the sale transaction and the income statement impact from a gain happening when the sale transaction happens. It also discloses on the balance sheet that the assets are being sold,
which indicates future cash inflows to users.

*Recommendation:* I recommend alternative 2 here if you have some idea of how much
you can sell the equipment for. This alternative provides the users with a better indica-
tion of the economic costs of what has occurred and a better ability to predict what is
coming in the next year.

These are the recommendations I have for you. Please note again that I have made
some significant assumptions in my analysis.[17] If those assumptions are incorrect, the
analysis on which they are based will likely have to be revisited. If that is the case,
please contact me.

---

[16] This issue could be missed entirely by a student who was not thorough in the information gathering at
the start of the case. The issue is given in one simple sentence in the case. However, we can provide value
to the client by informing her of the two reasonable treatments and what each will provide in terms of
information to the users.

[17] This is not simply a formality to cover ourselves, nor is it avoiding responsibility. It is very important to
remind the client — especially an unsophisticated one who comes to you with the assumption that
accounting provides cut-and-dried treatments in all situations — that your recommendations are valid only
in the context in which they are made.

# C H A P T E R  6

# INTRODUCTORY CASES

The cases in this book have been divided into three chapters — introductory, inter-mediate, and advanced. All of these cases could be used in an introductory finan-cial accounting course. The more advanced cases typically raise a broader range of issues or have more complex interactions among issues than the introductory cases. The advanced cases may also allow (without requiring) the application of more com-plex frameworks in generating alternative courses of action.

It is important to recognize, however, that even the introductory cases could be used in upper-year accounting courses. Because these cases involve the use of judg-ment, your analyses of them will change as your knowledge changes. At first you will analyze cases based on your general knowledge of society and business combined with your logic and common sense. As you develop more familiarity with the theories underlying business, economics, and financial accounting, you will be able to apply these frameworks to the cases to generate richer, better justified alternatives. As you gain knowledge of the current institutional basis of law, tax, and accounting, you will better understand the constraints under which financial reporting occurs and be able to further refine your recommendations to ensure that they can be implemented in a particular context. See Chapter 9 for further discussion of this.

There is an old joke about a professor who was accused of using the same exam questions year after year. The professor readily admitted that he did, but added: "I always change the answers!" I am sure you have looked back at either personal or academic things you have written and been amazed at how much your thinking has changed as you have gained in knowledge, experience, and maturity. A good case should allow for multiple analyses. Within a group of people at the same level of knowledge, a good case allows for differences of opinion about how to proceed. As people become more knowledgeable and more skilled at case analysis, their perspec-tives on cases will deepen, allowing more nuanced alternatives, better predictions of the consequences of each alternative, and the selection of recommendations that are more likely to achieve the client's objectives within the constraints imposed.

The purpose of case analysis is not to find the "right answer." It is first and fore-most to develop a process for thinking through the issues, developing alternatives, and presenting and defending your recommendations. When you finish a case analysis in the classroom, the test of the quality of the analysis is not whether you reached a consensus in the class, or whether your solution mirrored the analysis of your professor. The true test of a case analysis is whether you believe you have exhaustively identified the issues, explored a comprehensive range of alternatives, and heard persuasive arguments for a future course of action. A good case analysis should leave you thinking about the issues and how else you could have handled the situation. You may not leave the classroom with closure, but you can leave knowing that you have increased your ability to handle the ambiguities and challenges that make up business decision making.

# AYRGLEN

## *Kevin Markle*

AyrGlen Limited (AyrGlen) has been in business for over 40 years. It was started by David Ayr in 1963, and he was the sole shareholder until recently. AyrGlen manufactures and retails clothing; 80% of its business is women's fashion, and the remainder is men's and children's fashion. When it first started, 100% of AyrGlen's business was the manufacture of women's clothing. As the cost of labour continued to increase, the business gradually evolved, and now it is 70% retail and 30% manufacturing.

David Ayr retired from his active role as president of the company in November 2003. He will continue to be a 30% shareholder in the company. He has given 35% of the shares to each of his two sons, Alan and Bart, and has also given them operational control of the company.

Before David gave the shares to Alan and Bart, AyrGlen paid a dividend of $2,000,000 to David. In order to finance that dividend, AyrGlen had to obtain a loan from the bank. Before obtaining that loan, AyrGlen had no long-term debt. A condition of the loan is that AyrGlen must provide the bank with audited financial statements each year. AyrGlen has never had its statements audited before.

Alan and Bart have come to you because they are having trouble agreeing on how some things should be accounted for. Neither brother has any accounting training or experience. David had always handled all of the accounting for the company. Alan and Bart cannot agree on what is most important as they start out running the company. Alan is worried that things might not go that well when David is not actively involved, and he wants to rely on the financial statements as an indicator of the company's success. Bart thinks it is most important to defer as much tax as possible.

The Ayr brothers have asked you to review the accounting records of the company, identify any significant issues, and recommend policies. They may seek a second opinion, so they ask you to explain your recommendations fully.

It is now April 2004. You have reviewed the records and identified the following:

- The company has a December 31 year end.
- AyrGlen sells the women's clothing it manufactures to retail stores nationwide. The customer orders the goods; AyrGlen ships them within five business days of the order and includes an invoice with the shipment which requires the customer to pay within 60 days. Ninety percent of all invoices are paid within 60 days; 2% of all invoices are never paid. Revenue has always been recorded on collection of cash.
- In January 2004, Alan and Bart made their first big operational decision when they decided to enrol AyrGlen in a retailers' association. AyrGlen was required to pay an initiation fee of $150,000 and will be required to pay annual dues of $10,000 in January of each year. Membership in the association entitles AyrGlen to discounts on advertising in the association magazine, promotion on the association website, and free access to all association-sponsored trade shows and conventions. Alan and Bart

have decided to give the association a try but are unsure of how long they will continue the membership.

- Each March, AyrGlen goes through its retail stock and pulls out all items that have been on the shelf for 18 months or more. It gives these clothes to local and international charities that help the less fortunate. No journal entry is made when this happens. AyrGlen uses a periodic inventory system.

- For the goods it manufactures and sells to retail stores, AyrGlen allows its customers to return goods for a credit towards future purchases for a period of 90 days from receipt of goods. AyrGlen is not usually able to resell the returned goods. These returns have always been recorded only when the return is made by the customer.

- AyrGlen owns the building that houses both its manufacturing facility and its retail store. The building is more than 50 years old, has required some extensive work over the past couple of years, and will likely require more work in the next several years. The building is in a great location and is a landmark in the town, so the brothers intend to spend whatever is necessary in order to prolong its life for many years. All work done on the building is expensed as repairs and maintenance when it is done.

## Required

Prepare the report for Alan and Bart Ayr.

# SWEET CHEEKS LIMITED

## *Arthur R. Guimaraes*

Ana, a businesswoman, is preparing to start a private company, Sweet Cheeks Limited (SCL). She will have no time to spend managing SCL, as she has her own tax practice. She will, however, be the 100% owner. She will not be active in SCL's day-to-day operations, but she has already hand-picked her management team, who will be rewarded by a bonus — 30% of their salary — based on their ability to reduce taxes payable. This is her business idea:

SCL will be a travel company that offers high-end vacation packages (approximately $10,000 per package, with 10,000 package sales expected in year 1). These will normally involve cruising the Mediterranean or the Caribbean for one month. These packages will be sold through travel agents. The payment schedule for these packages will be as follows:

- On sale of the package — 20% paid to the travel agent and then forwarded to SCL;
- Two weeks before trip – 50% paid to the travel agent and then forwarded to SCL; *and*
- At end of trip – 30% paid to the travel agent and then forwarded to SCL.

Industry information states that owing to difficult economic times, bad debts in the travel agency business have been increasing lately. Some travel agents may have to declare bankruptcy; if they do, any funds in transit will not be not received by the cruise company. In the prior year, such funds amounted to 7% of sales.

SCL will have to purchase two large cruise ships, each costing $25 million. This will require financing. Ana intends to borrow funds from her banker, Mr. Naïf, whose lending decision will be based primarily on the company's ability to maximize its income. Ana is confident that she will be able to secure a loan of at least $75 million — sufficient to start SCL's operations. The two ships will be purchased at the same time and will likely have a useful life of approximately 30 years. She expects that each ship will make 10 round trips per year and require roughly five days' maintenance between trips.

Ana has asked your firm, CWP, to prepare a report on accounting policies. She requires a detailed report on the potential accounting issues and their impact on the key users of SCL's financial statements.

## Required

Prepare a detailed report for Ana that recommends accounting policies.

# WIND JAMMER INC.

### *K. Bewley*

Wind Jammer Inc. (WJI) was incorporated in 2003 by its sole shareholder, Jie Whaler. WJI operates a yacht that provides tours of Toronto Harbour. The yacht can also be rented by private groups on a per hour basis. During September 2003, its first month of operation, the following transactions and events occurred.

*September 1:* WJI was incorporated and Jie Whaler contributed $275,000 cash in exchange for 100 common shares of the company.

*September 2:* Purchased a yacht, the *Wind Jammer XL*, for $300,000, paying $200,000 in cash and the remainder as a loan payable to the seller of the boat. Interest on the loan is 12%, due monthly starting September 30, 2003. The loan must be repaid in full on August 31, 2006.

*September 2:* The seller has agreed to rent a docking space to WJI for $300 per month. WJI paid $1,500 for docking rights up to the end of February 2004.

*September 3:* Insurance is arranged. The monthly premium of $370 is payable on the 15th of each month, and the first payment is made on September 15, 2004.

*September 4:* WJI paid $4,500 for lumber and supplies to construct a booth for selling tickets at the dock. Leftover lumber worth about $2,000 was taken to Jie Whaler's home in Oakville to be used to build a deck.

*September 4:* WJI purchased $1,650 worth of fuel, and life jackets and other safety supplies worth $1,900, all on credit.

*September 15:* WJI received a deposit of $3,000 from a customer, who wants to rent the boat for a company party on October 2, 2003. The full price of the rental will be $6,000.

*September 1–30:* Sales for the month were:

- Rentals paid in cash = $5,600
- Rentals on credit (still outstanding at September 30th) = $970
- Tour tickets paid for in cash — $8,800. $550 worth of the tour tickets were unused as of the end of September.

*September 30:* WJI paid $8,000 to Jie Whaler as a salary, and $4,600 to employees for the month's wages.

Additional information:

- About half the fuel is remaining at the end of September.
- A lawyer's bill for $1,100 for incorporating the company is received on October 2.

## Required

1. Assume the role of WJI's accountant and provide journal entries for the above transactions and events. Ignore all taxes. Explain each entry.
2. Assume the role of a banker. WJI applies to your bank for a $100,000 loan on October 4, 2003. Which financial statements would you request from WJI, and why? Would you approve the loan? Explain the information you use and the reasons for your decision.

# HEALTHY DAIRY

## Elizabeth Farrell

Healthy Dairy Incorporated (HDI) is a private company that raises milking cows fed only with organic feed. It also has a dairy operation that produces organic milk and other dairy products, such as ice cream. Organic dairy products — milk, for example — have a shelf life of 60 days. All the common shares of HDI are owned by two individuals, Lee and Marissa. Lee operates the organic dairy operations and Marissa runs the organic farming operations. Lee has a combination business and agricultural degree from the University of Guelph; so does Marissa. With the current trend towards healthy eating and organic products, they hope to go public soon.

HDI has a bank loan with an agricultural co-op. The loan requires audited financial statements and a maximum debt-to-equity ratio and has a covenant restricting the distribution of dividends if the loan requirements are not met. Lee and Marissa anticipate that in 2005 these covenants will be met.

HDI has been extremely profitable for the past three years, with many people now recognizing the importance of a healthy lifestyle. Additional financing has been required only to expand the business so that it can keep up with the demand for its products.

The income tax rate in 2005 is 40% and the incremental borrowing rate is 10%.

HDI has hired you to run its financial operations. The owners have asked you to recommend accounting policies for the following issues:

1. HDI received a government grant from the Ministry of Agriculture in 2005 for the purchase of new computers to track information on each cow. As a condition of the grant, for the next three years HDI must provide the government with audited financial statements and meet all government regulations to be certified organic. If these conditions are met, the loan will not need to be paid back; if the conditions are not met, the loan and interest will be repayable.

2. In January 2005, HDI purchased a small dairy farm, Moo Limited (ML), in order to obtain sufficient milk to meet the increased demand for its organic products. The dairy industry is controlled by milk quotas. These quotas guarantee HDI a minimum price for its milk and are renewable indefinitely. HDI paid $5 million for ML. The values of ML's assets and liabilities were:

|  | Book value | Fair value |
|---|---|---|
| Cattle | $ 20,000 | $ 500,000 |
| Farm equipment | 10,000 | 80,000 |
| Land | 5,000 | 1,200,000 |
| Liabilities | 1,000,000 | 1,000,000 |

3. In 2005, HDI implemented a new computer system that tracks the amount of milk each cow produces, the amount it eats, and any medications it receives. As part of the government's organic certification process, records must be kept of the feed the cows

eat and the medications they take. They must be fed only organic feed (i.e., feeds untouched by pesticides or chemicals), and they must not be given any antibiotics or growth hormones. A computer record can be printed off for each cow. Besides new computers costing $100,000, HDI purchased an existing computer program for $10,000, which Marissa adapted and redesigned to meet HDI's needs. The only cost involved was her time. Other farms have offered to lease this software from her. HDI has patented this software at a cost of $1,000. Marissa anticipates revenues of over $400,000 from the lease of this software internationally.

4. At the start of 2005, HDI decided to go 100% organic. To this end, Lee and Marissa needed to sell any cows that had not been raised solely on organic feed. These cows were sold to other farms for $2 million. Each year some of the cows for the farm are purchased from breeders; others are raised on the farm. About 20% of the cows are for breeding purposes; the other 80% are for milking. It takes approximately two years from the time a calf is born until it can produce milk. Before 2005, all male cows (which of course are not milked) were sold at birth. Now these cows are being raised on the farm as beef cattle. Organic beef is also in high demand.

5. In 2005, owing to a mad cow scare on a nearby farm, the government compelled HDI to destroy all its beef cattle. The fair value of the cattle destroyed was $1.5 million. This cost was not covered by insurance or the government.

6. HDI's dairy products are shipped to supermarkets and stores that sell organic products. These outlets are guaranteed that if they cannot sell the products within 30 days they can be shipped back to HDI. Organic products are currently high in demand. HDI has trouble meeting all its orders and often runs out of inventory.

7. On January 1, 2005, HDI signed a lease agreement with Trucks Incorporated for delivery trucks. Each truck has a list price of $35,500. The annual lease payment per truck, due each December 31, is $10,000. The lease is for four years. If more than 5000 km are put on the truck in one year, a payment of $0.30 per kilometre must be paid in addition to the lease payment. All maintenance costs are covered by warranty. At the end of the four years, HDI may renew the lease at the "black book" value (i.e., the market rate). Each truck has an estimated life of six years. If HDI does not renew the lease, the truck will be returned to Trucks Incorporated, which will either sell the truck or lease it again.

## Required

Provide a report outlining your recommendations on accounting policies to Lee and Marissa.

# CRANBERRY MARSH

## *Elizabeth Farrell*

Cranberry Marsh Incorporated (CMI) is a private corporation that started operations in the 1950s as a cranberry marsh. It was founded by two brothers, Jim and Peter Red. All of the common shares are currently owned by the brothers. The cranberries are sold to businesses wholesale as well as to customers on the farm. In addition, cranberry products — jams, jellies, and the like — are sold in a small store on the farm.

A farmers' co-op (FCB) lends Jim and Peter money at the low interest rate of 6%. With their type of operation, if they went to a bank to borrow money or enter a lease agreement, the current market rate would be 10%. In years when weather conditions result in a poor harvest, the FCB will provide additional loans as needed and suspend existing loan payments for a year. The FCB requires financial statements on an annual basis to support these loans but does not require an audit.

To reduce the risk of a bad year from weather and to address the seasonal nature of the business, Jim decided at the beginning of 2005 to launch a new business venture — making and selling fruit wine. The start-up period to get a winery off the ground is approximately two years. Peter disagreed with this business decision. The brothers agreed that at the end of 2005 Peter would retire from the business. Since there was no ready market for the shares of CMI, the value of Peter's investment would be determined based on the December 31, 2005, financial statements. Peter would receive cash for his shares based on that value. The necessary cash would be obtained from the sale of excess land. Peter would also receive 40% of net income before extraordinary items for the next three years.

To finance the wine-making venture, CMI issued preferred shares, with the dividends payable in bottles of wine rather than cash. The amount of the dividend (bottles of wine) would depend on the level of income achieved in a year. The preferred shareholders required as part of their share purchase that audited financial statements be provided by CMI. In addition, CMI received a forgivable loan from the government. This loan stipulated that a certain percentage of Ontario-grown fruit must be used in the production of the wine; also, five employees would have to be hired full-time for five years.

CMI has no desire to go public.

You have been hired by Jim Red to help him decide on the accounting policies for 2005. In the past, financial statements have been prepared only for the bank and for income tax purposes. The following items require accounting policies for 2005:

1. On the farm, an existing building was converted for use in filtering, aging, and storing the wine. Its existing doors were modified to ensure that a constant temperature would be maintained. The cost to convert the building was $2 million, which included:

   - interest costs of financing from FCB;
   - renovations to the building;
   - salaries of Jim and Peter Red; *and*
   - overhead costs.

2. CMI signed an agreement to purchase 50 oak barrels to age the wine in. These barrels, which are imported from France, cost $200 each and last for five years.
3. CMI purchased 100% of the common shares of a small winery for $4 million. It received the following as part of the purchase:

|                       | Cost          | Fair market value |
|-----------------------|---------------|-------------------|
| Wine making equipment | $1.5 million  | $2 million        |

In addition to the equipment, CMI received the following. First, an exclusive employment contract with Ms. Verina, one of the top winemakers in Ontario. She agreed to stay with CMI for five years. Second, the rights to the winery's award-winning recipes for fruit wines. Third, the rights to a government licence to sell wine in Ontario. These licences are difficult to obtain, since only a limited number are provided in Ontario.

4. To increase the public's awareness of the new winery and the existing farm operations, CSI developed a website. Costs were incurred in 2005 for the following items:

- upgrades to the current computer system;
- the design of graphics for the website;
- the design of a new logo for the farm and winery operations; *and*
- registration of the Internet domain name.

5. To provide enough fruit for winemaking, CMI purchased more vines from a cranberry farm in Halifax. To save cash, it exchanged the vines for some excess farm equipment. CMI paid $50,000 to ship the vines from Halifax. Once the vines are planted, if properly maintained they will produce fruit indefinitely.
6. CMI has always used the taxes-payable method for income taxes.
7. CMI anticipates losses of $1,000,000 in 2005 and $400,000 in 2006. The losses reflect the start-up period for the winemaking business. After that, large profits are anticipated. Fruit wine and cranberries in general are popular now and are expected to become more so.

## Required

Provide a report outlining your recommendations on accounting policies to Jim Red.

# LOADDOWN.COM

## *Kevin Markle*

Your friend, Heza Nerd, has jumped on the music-downloading bandwagon and come up with a concept that he believes can make him a lot of money. He has set up a website — Loaddown.com — that people can visit to download songs for a small fee. After signing up, the user receives a login name and password and is allowed to download any five songs for free. After that, there are three subscription plans:

1. Pay as you go — The user's account is charged $1 for every song downloaded from the site.
2. Monthly — For $50 per month, the user can download up to 75 songs per month. For the 76th song and beyond, the charge is $1 per song.
3. Annual — For $500 per year, the user can download up to 1,000 songs per year.

The monthly and annual plans must be paid in full up front before the first song can be downloaded.

Loaddown.com has signed a deal with a major music distributor to use its songs exclusively. Loaddown.com will pay a monthly fee of $20,000 on the 1st of every month as well as a per song fee of $0.30 for every song downloaded. The per song fee will be payable to the distributor on the 15th of each month and will pay for the songs downloaded the previous month (i.e., the February 15 bill will be for songs downloaded in January).

To set up the site, Heza had to borrow $100,000 from the bank. Most of this loan was spent buying the necessary hardware and paying the salaries of the software developers he had to hire. Because Heza is a computer guy with no background in running a business, he hired Jim Dandy, an MBA graduate, to manage the operations. Jim believes so strongly in the venture that he has agreed to a compensation package consisting of a minimal salary plus a bonus based on the net income number on the annual income statement.

## Required

Heza has contacted you for help in establishing some policies to guide the accounting for Loaddown.com. Specifically, he wants you to answer the following questions:

1. Who will be the main users of Loaddown.com's financial statements? What will each use the financial statements for?
2. What are the objectives of each of the users identified in 1?
3. What revenue and expense recognition policies would satisfy each of the objectives in 2?
4. Which of the policies in 3 would be most appropriate for Loaddown.com? Explain why.

# TORONTO AUTUMN LEAVES

## *Kevin Markle*

A new hockey team, the Toronto Autumn Leaves (The Leaves), has obtained formal approval to join the National Hockey League. The Leaves are owned by a corporation (TAL Inc.) owned by you and three friends (25% each). Each of you has put in $100 in exchange for 25 of the 100 shares outstanding. The funds required to launch the team were borrowed by TAL from a bank. The owners are considering issuing additional shares as a source of capital. You will be active in the management of the corporation; the other three owners will not be. You will be compensated with a market-value salary plus a bonus of 10% of reported net income. The bank has asked for audited annual financial statements.

With TAL Inc.'s first year end (December 31, 2002) quickly approaching, the company needs to set some accounting policies that will guide the preparation of financial statements. The following issues have been identified:

1. The Leaves will play their home games in a new arena called The Compost, which is owned by an unrelated company. The Compost will own and administer the concession sales (food and drinks, etc.). For each home game TAL will receive either (1) 20% of the net concession sales or (2) $10,000, whichever is more. The amount will be payable to TAL Inc. two weeks after each game. In determining when to recognize this revenue, the owners are most concerned about amounts related to games in the last two weeks of December.

2. TAL Inc. has entered into an exclusive licensing agreement with Neek Inc., a sports equipment manufacturer. The agreement requires Neek to pay TAL $600,000 on July 1 and January 1 of each year for the right to produce and sell equipment and clothing with The Leaves' logo on it. In addition, Neek is required to pay 10% of the gross sales of the merchandise to TAL each month. (Consider the semiannual payments and the monthly commissions separately.)

3. The team has been able to persuade Wayne Gretzky to end his retirement and play for the team. As soon as this announcement was made, season's ticket subscriptions sold out. Gretzky's contract with The Leaves is for three years. He was paid a signing bonus of $3 million when the contract was signed on October 14, 2002. Gretzky intends to play for three years but has been having back problems that will keep him out of the lineup for the first month of the season. Under no circumstances will he be required to repay a portion of the signing bonus.

The other owners have asked you to prepare a report in which you identify possible accounting treatments for each of the issues and recommend how each should be treated.

## Required

Prepare the report requested by the other owners. Your report should:

(a) identify the likely users of the financial statements and describe the uses they will have for the statements;

(b) explain the possible objectives of financial reporting, and rank the objectives; *and*

(c) discuss reasonable alternative treatments for the accounting issues and recommend how TAL should account for each issue. Your discussion and recommendations should consider any relevant constraints, facts, and objectives.

# MUKLUK LIMITED

## *K. Bewley*

MukLuk Limited (MukLuk), a private company near Anchorage, Alaska, manufactures winter boots. The majority shareholders are members of a family that has owned the company for three generations; the company's dividends are their main source of income. MukLuk's managers are not family members; they are paid in salaries and bonuses based on pretax profits and hold small amounts of nonvoting shares.

In April 2003, MukLuk's new vice-president of marketing (a recent MBA graduate) convinced one of the company's regular customers, SL Inc. (SLI) to feature MukLuk's boots as part of a special early-winter promotion. SLI is chain of retail sporting goods stores. This will allow MukLuk to manufacture the boots at a time when its factory usually has excess capacity, and thus increase the overall efficiency of MukLuk's operations. The order is for 20,000 pairs of boots, to be delivered as follows:

8,000 pairs on October 10
5,000 pairs on November 10
5,000 pairs on December 10
2,000 pairs on January 10

The SLI contract will set out the selection of sizes it will require and the selling price. SLI will be required to pay within 30 days of receiving each delivery. Since April to June tends to be a slow time in the factory, MukLuk's managers plan to produce the 20,000 pairs during April and May and store the boots in a rented warehouse until delivery. The managers expect that their new marketing VP will bring in additional orders for later in the year; they will then have capacity in June to accept these orders as well. MukLuk typically has little or no bank debt, but the decision to manufacture this large order early will require the company to borrow cash from the bank so that it will be able to finance production and still pay out regular annual dividends to shareholders. The company has a June 30 year end.

## Required

1. Identify three likely objectives of accounting for MukLuk's June 30, 2003, financial statements, and explain why you think each is likely.
2. At what point(s) in time could revenue be recognized in this situation? On what facts and constraints does this depend?
3. Assume the role of MukLuk's chief financial officer. The president of the company has not yet signed the SLI contract and has come to you with a question about the deal. "This is a fantastic sale and the whole management team is really looking forward to getting a huge bonus for earning these profits in the June 30, 2003, year! When can we expect to receive our bonus cheques?" What factors would need to be included in the contract for the managers' bonus to include the SLI sale in 2003?

# PCC INC.

## *K. Bewley*

PCC Inc. is an importer and distributor of computer chips (integrated circuits used in computers). PCC started business this year. During its first year, 2000, PCC received three large shipments of chips from suppliers in Asia and sold those chips to small computer assemblers and retailers. PCC employs several buyers and salespeople. During the company's first year the cost of chips fell substantially, but its selling prices so far have declined only slightly. Inventory and preliminary financial information related to PCC are given below.

## Inventory Information

**Inventory purchased during the year 2000:**

| | | |
|---|---|---|
| Purchase 1 | January 1 | 1,000 chips at $50 each |
| Purchase 2 | June 30 | 1,000 chips at $40 each |
| Purchase 3 | September 30 | 1,000 chips at $32 each |

**Sales during 2000:**

| | |
|---|---|
| January to June | 800 chips at $100 each |
| July to September | 700 chips at $100 each |
| November and December | 200 chips at $90 each |

On hand at year end:       1,300 chips

## Preliminary Financial Information

**Year ended December 31, 2000**

| | |
|---|---:|
| Assets | |
| Cash | $  13 |
| Accounts receivable | 35 |
| Inventory | 44 |
| Prepaid expenses | 18 |
| Equipment, at cost | 100 |
| Less accumulated amortization | <u>10</u> |
| Equipment, net book value | <u>90</u> |
| Total assets | $ <u>200</u> |
| | |
| Liabilities | |
| Accounts payable | $  22 |
| Bank Loan — long-term | 40 |
| Shareholder's equity | |
| Common shares issued | 130 |
| Retained earnings | <u>8</u> |
| Total liabilities and shareholder's equity | $ <u>200</u> |

| Sales | $ 168 |
|---|---|
| Cost of sales | 78 |
| Gross profit | 90 |
| Operating expenses | 30 |
| Selling expenses | 36 |
| Amortization expense | 10 |
| Interest expense | 4 |
| Net income before income taxes | 10 |
| Income taxes | 2 |
| Net income | $    8 |

## Required

Answer the following, stating any assumptions you make.

1. Which inventory costing method has been used to prepare the preliminary financial information given below, FIFO or LIFO? How can you tell?
2. Prepare a cash flow statement for the year ended December 31, 2000. Identify cash flows relating to operating, investing, and financing activities, and comment on the information this statement provides.
3. What would be the impact on the financial statements of changing from one inventory costing method (i.e., FIFO or LIFO) to the other, and of applying the lower of cost and market rule? Consider the likely users and objectives of accounting in this situation.

# REENGINEERING INC.

## K. Bewley

Reengineering Inc. (RI) is a private corporation that provides consulting services on systems redesign and implementation for a variety of manufacturing and service business clients. It is owned by its four managers, each of whom holds 25% of the company's common shares. During the 1990s the company grew quickly and financed this growth through a bank operating line of credit. This line of credit can be called on to cover cash shortages up to a maximum of $1,000,000. The bank requires monthly income statements and a full set of financial statements annually, prepared in accordance with GAAP, to support this operating line. The banking agreement also includes covenants that require RI to maintain a minimum working capital ratio of $2:1$. A further restriction is that no payments can be made to shareholders if the line of credit reaches $1,000,000 or if the working capital ratio falls below $2:1$.

You are an accounting advisor to RI. It is now December 2001. You are reviewing the company's draft financial statements for its October 31, 2001, year end and learn the following:

- Accounts receivable of $5,000,000 include $3,000,000 for a large contract obtained in early October 2001. Several consultants have been working on the contract, but no system is in place for keeping track of the time spent on the project. The total contract is estimated to be $3,600,000. It is expected that it will take about one year to complete.
- Consultants are required to travel to sell consulting contracts to clients in various parts of the world. The consultants submit claims for travel expenses after they return. One of the consultants has just submitted a claim for $50,000 for travel over the period July to October 2001. No accrual had been made for these expenses.
- In September RI had a cash shortfall of $1,100,000 after writing its payroll cheques for employees. To avoid exceeding the bank line of credit, one of the shareholders lent $100,000 to RI. The shareholders have not paid their own salaries since August, as this would put them in excess of their line of credit.

## Required

Advise RI's management on how to account for the above items. Provide other advice as appropriate.

# ROBBIN INC.

## *K. Bewley*

Robbin Inc., a public company, is an electronic goods retailer. At the start of the current fiscal year Robbin changed from selling all of its products with an optional third-party extended service plan (warranty) to selling an in-house extended service plan as part of the normal retail selling price of the product. Thus the revenue stream for the service plan changed from being a commission from a third-party vendor, who took full responsibility for doing the actual service work, to revenue being received as part of Robbin's selling price and Robbin accepting full responsibility for service.

Robbin's management wanted to continue to recognize all service revenue when the product was sold despite the change in how Robbin provides service. Robbin's auditor objected to management's accounting policy choice, arguing that it did not reflect the substance of the transaction stream. The auditor's proposed accounting policy would lead to a material change in Robbin's financial statements, so the auditor is insisting that management accept the change.

## Required

Assume the role of an accounting advisor to Robbin's management.

1. Describe the impact the proposed change in accounting policy would have on Robbin's assets, liabilities, revenues, and expenses.
2. Analyze the options for accounting for Robbin's extended service transactions, and provide a recommendation.

# NEW AGE SPIRITUAL ACADEMY

## *V. Umashanker Trivedi*

New Age Spiritual Academy (NASA) is a not-for-profit religious organization recognized as a charitable organization by the government. As a charity, all of its activities that are related to its main objective are exempt from taxation. However, NASA also conducts a few activities that do make a profit, and it has to pay taxes on these. NASA is run by volunteers, some of whom form its board of directors. A paid manager was hired in the middle of the year when the workload became too much for the volunteers.

NASA is funded mainly through donations obtained from its members. Its principal asset is a huge building with spacious parking facilities. The building contains a large meeting room on the ground floor and a dining hall with adjacent kitchen facilities in the basement. The building is located in a busy part of town. An annual report of NASA's activities has to be issued to all its members, who are also its main donors. Donations and almost all the revenues are received in cash. NASA, being a charitable organization, is also required to submit its annual report to the government. However, the government has not specified any particular accounting method to be used for the annual report submitted to it.

Following are details of NASA's various activities:

## Revenues from Not-for-Profit Activities

- Annual fundraising dinner, annual arts and crafts sale, and annual bake sale.
- Weekly fundraising at prayer time.
- Annual memberships, life memberships, and miscellaneous receipts.
- Annual matching grant by government (all not-for-profit revenues matched dollar for dollar).

## Revenues from For-Profit Activities (Activities Deemed to Be for Profit by the Tax Authority)

- *Renting of parking lot* — NASA has contracted out the right to collect parking fees during weekdays between 7 a.m. and 5 p.m. The contractor has agreed to pay NASA a lump sum amount for obtaining this right, payable in 12 monthly instalments. The contractor is free to charge any amount to his customers. All repair and maintenance costs in relation to the parking lot are to be borne by NASA.
- *Renting of hall* — The hall and the parking lot are used by the members on Sunday mornings for prayer meetings. The building and the parking lot are rented out for various functions after 5 p.m. on weekdays, all day on Saturdays, and after 12 noon on Sundays.

## NASA has various expenses, including the following:

- Weekly cleaning of parking lot and building.
- Heating and lighting.

- Repairs and maintenance of building.
- Repairs and maintenance of furniture and fixtures in the hall and dining hall, and of utensils and equipment in the kitchen.
- Weekly prayers (related costs).
- Costs related to various festivals celebrated during the year.
- Costs related to the annual events — fundraising dinner, arts and crafts sale, bake sale, and so on. These activities are held in venues other than the building, typically in a hotel.
- The mortgage held by a local credit union, obtained to fund the purchase of the premises.

Some members have voiced concern about the efficiency and effectiveness of the board of directors. Also, they are not sure whether the various annual events are effective and whether the organization makes any profits from these.

## Required

The board of directors has learned that you are taking accounting courses and believe you are eminently qualified to advise them. Specifically, they want you to advise them what accounting policies they ought to be following and what records they ought to be keeping. Please oblige the board.

# HARRINGTON BOOKS

## V. Umashanker Trivedi

Peter Harrington inherited a collection of rare and possibly valuable books on Eastern religion from his father, who had been well connected in publishing circles. When the question of what to do with the books arose, he thought of using his father's contacts to start a bookstore. His intention was to sell the books he had inherited as well as other books published by his contacts. So he obtained a two-year lease on a store in a strip mall and started his bookstore, which he named Harrington Books. He also established a website, Harrington-Books.com, to advertise his store and to sell books over the Internet. Further details about the business during the first year of its operations are provided below:

- Peter paid lump sum amounts to various publishers to obtain the sole distributorship rights to books published by these publishers for specified periods of time, these being typically in the range of two to five years. Peter believes that on average, these distributorships will be profitable. However, he cannot predict what the sales patterns for these books will be.
- Peter also paid lump sum amounts to various authors to obtain the copyright to their books. These copyrights entitle Peter to obtain royalties from sales of those books from the publisher for the life of the copyright. At this time, Peter cannot predict which of the books he owns the copyrights for will sell well and which will not; nor can he predict the sales patterns for these books. Peter stocks the books for which he holds copyright in his store, and intends to sell them himself at the store and over the Internet.
- Peter incurred a one-time website development cost to set up the website. He has also entered into a two-year agreement with a hosting company, which will "post" his website. Under agreement with the host, monthly charges are due and payable at the beginning of each month.
- Though Peter spends a considerable amount of his spare time running the store (he holds a full-time job elsewhere), he has hired a full-time manager. The manager receives a fixed monthly salary plus a bonus based on year-end profits. Peter has chosen not to draw a salary from the store.
- Peter uses the warehouse at the back of his bookstore to hold the inventory of books he has purchased. He has decided to offer rebates and discounts on those books in his inventory that have been moving slowly over the previous six months.
- Peter also distributes books to other booksellers throughout the country. These booksellers are paid a commission for each book they sell. They can return unsold books at any time. All transportation costs are borne by Peter.
- Peter came up with a marketing strategy whereby people can buy six books of their choice for a dollar. However, to take advantage of this offer, they must buy six more books at their regular prices in the following two years. This strategy has been a huge success.

- Peter has financed his sole distributorships, his copyrights to various books, and the purchase of books for his inventory by using a line of credit from one of the major banks. The bank has provided this line of credit using the inventory, the distributorship rights, and the copyrights as collateral.
- Harrington Books is a sole proprietorship.

## Required

Advise Peter on appropriate accounting policies and accounting records in relation to Harrington Books.

# HAPPY TIMES RETIREMENT HOMES LIMITED

## *Dilsat Tuna*

Happy Times Retirement Homes Limited (HTL) is a private company that is currently wholly owned by a local family. HTL is in the business of buying land and building retirement homes. Over the years it has been involved in two separate activities, one being the purchase of land for development into retirement homes, the other being the operation of retirement homes. In some cases HTL buys the land and waits to sell it to a company that wants to build a retirement home. In other cases it buys the land and holds it until the owners see fit to build a retirement home. HTL sometimes builds and operates the retirement homes.

HTL's owners are heavily involved in the business and are always "scoping out" new parcels of desirable land. For many years HTL has been acquiring land with scenic views and other natural attributes. Currently the company owns many desirable pieces of land, which it has recorded on its books at cost.

Owing to the aging population, there has been increased interest in the "retirement residences/retirement care" industry. HTL's owners have recently been approached by an American company, Greener Pastures Retirement Communities Incorporated (GPI). GPI has offered to purchase HTL and has proposed a price based on HTL's net income for the 2004 year end based on GAAP financial statements. The final details of the proposal have not been decided on; neither has the timing. It appears that although GPI is not in a hurry to decide, it would like to enter the Canadian market as soon as possible. In fact, GPI has told HTL's owners that "even if HTL does not want to sell the whole company to GPI, we would like to consider other ways that we can do business with HTL to enter the Canadian market."

It is now September 2004. HTL's owners have asked you to provide a report with recommendations for accounting policies for the December 31, 2004, year end. They have also asked you to respond to GPI's question regarding "other ways that they can do business with HTL to enter the Canadian market." You have been provided with the following information to assist in your analysis:

1. At the beginning of 2004, HTL purchased a large parcel of land from the Government of Canada for $3.5 million. Before engineers and architects could plan the proposed retirement home, HTL had to spend thousands of dollars "readying" the land for planning. Prior to the design stage the company hires engineers and architects, as well as consultants who assess whether a retirement home would be feasible. In the past these costs have been expensed as incurred. The following are some of these costs:

   - Travel costs of approximately $85,000 for the professionals to visit the site.
   - Professional fees charged by the engineers, architects, and other consultants of approximately $320,000.

2. Although in general HTL's business is growing, the company has found that some of the retirement homes it has been operating for years are not performing as well as the newer homes. The owners have decided that all retirement homes more than 10 years old are to be part of a major restructuring program. This program will be aimed at managing these homes more efficiently. As is the case with many restructuring programs, HTL plans to reduce staff levels. It is estimated that the cost of the anticipated terminations will be between $1.2 to 2.6 million. These costs are expected to be incurred at the end of 2004 and throughout the 2005 fiscal year.

3. During 2004, HTL opened a new retirement home in Cambridge, Ontario. The same year, to attract new residents and employees, HTL spent $370,000 on an advertising program. The advertising costs consisted of the following:

   - $290,000 for television ads to attract new residents. These ads will continue until the retirement home is 90% occupied. HTL reached an agreement with the ad agency that the time period could range anywhere from a minimum of one to a maximum of three years or until the home was 90% occupied, whichever was sooner.
   - $55,000 was spent on a newspaper ad. This full-page ad ran in the local papers and in some high-profile newspapers throughout southwestern Ontario for a total of three Sundays in February and March 2004.
   - $25,000 was spent on classified ads to attract new employees to the retirement home. These ads ran in the local newspapers for eight weeks.

4. As part of the grand opening of the Cambridge retirement home, HTL ran a promotion whereby customers could "reserve" the suite of their choice with a one-time deposit of $10,000. This promotion was open to people over 50 who were not yet ready to reside in a retirement home. This reservation would give the customers priority status on a "waiting list." On deciding to reside at the Cambridge retirement home, the customer would be able to use the $10,000 towards rent. The deposit would be refundable at any time within one year of signing the deposit agreement. The promotion was a huge success, and HTL collected $1.3 million in deposits.

## Required

Provide the requested report for the owners.

# BBEAN COFFEE INC.

## *K. Bewley*

BBean Coffee Inc. is a public company that sells coffee shop franchises and provides ongoing support and marketing services to franchise purchasers. In the beginning, BBean only sold large coffee shop franchises in the downtowns of major cities. Franchises were sold for $400,000, with the purchaser arranging its own financing for this amount. At the start of the current fiscal year, BBean recognized that the large urban centres were becoming saturated with large coffee shops, so it began selling smaller franchises, which were to be set up in suburban shopping centres and smaller cities. The smaller franchises were sold for $300,000, with $100,000 payable immediately and the balance due in four annual instalments of $50,000. BBean's management wishes to continue with its accounting policy of recognizing the total franchise selling price immediately when the franchise is sold.

BBean's auditor is objecting to management's choice of accounting policy; in her view it no longer reflects the substance of the transaction stream and overstates BBean's earnings by a material amount. The auditor is insisting that management change to a more appropriate accounting policy.

## Required

Assume the role of an accounting advisor to BBean's management.

1. Analyze the options for accounting for BBean's franchise sale transactions and provide a recommendation.
2. Describe the impact your recommended change in accounting policy would have on BBean's assets, liabilities, revenues, expenses, and earnings.

# PARSONS' PARTS INC.

### Kevin Markle

Parsons' Parts Inc. (PPI) is a privately owned family business that manufactures parts for the automotive industry. The company has been in business for over 30 years and has consistently generated net income between $100,000 and $300,000 each year. The family's philosophy has always been to finance growth internally; for this reason they have never taken dividends out of the company.

Robyn Parsons, the granddaughter of the company's founder, took over its management in late 2002. At that time she decided the moment was right to expand the company at a faster pace. To that end, on January 1, 2003, PPI issued a $2,000,000 bond to a private investor, Terrence Barnsworth. The bond had a coupon rate of 10%, called for interest payments to be made annually at the end of each year, and had a maturity date of December 31, 2014. Instead of making the bond retractable, Mr. Barnsworth insisted that if the company's debt-to-equity ratio (total liabilities to total equity) exceeded 2.5:1 on any of its annual financial statements, a penalty of $500,000 would be payable to him.

At the time the loan agreement was made, Robyn explained to Barnsworth that the company's financial statements were produced mainly for internal purposes. The company's overall policy had always been to apply GAAP, but departures from GAAP were made when the resulting information would be more useful for internal purposes. Barnsworth agreed to use the internal statements but insisted that he (or his representative) be allowed to review the statements each year to ensure that no accounting choices had been made solely to manipulate the debt-to-equity ratio. He and Robyn will meet each year to review the statements. Any disagreements over the numbers that cannot be settled by the two of them will be settled by an independent arbitrator. They have agreed that any tax effects can be left out of the discussion.

It is now February 2004. Mr. Barnsworth has hired you, an accountant, as his representative and asked you to review PPI's December 31, 2003, draft financial statements. He wants you to prepare a report that identifies pertinent issues and recommends ways to deal with them. He also wants you to recalculate the debt-to-equity ratio based on any changes you recommend. Finally, he wants supporting reasoning for your recommendations that he can bring to his discussions with Robyn. He will be taking your report into his meeting with her and so would like it to prepare him for what she might say about the issues.

You have reviewed the files of PPI and have found the following:

1. Summarized balance sheets for the fiscal years ended December 31:

|  | 2003 (draft) | 2002 | 2001 |
| --- | --- | --- | --- |
| Total assets | 7,500,000 | 5,000,000 | 4,500,000 |
| Total liabilities | 4,500,000 | 2,400,000 | 2,200,000 |
| Capital stock | 1,000 | 1,000 | 1,000 |
| Retained earnings | 2,999,000 | 2,599,000 | 2,299,000 |
| Total shareholders' equity | 3,000,000 | 2,600,000 | 2,300,000 |

2. In October 2003 one of PPI's long-standing customers placed a large order for parts to be delivered in equal proportions in December 2003 and January 2004. The total price of the order was $750,000 for 42,000 parts. As is normal with this customer, the full price was paid in advance. For many years, PPI had recognized revenue when parts are shipped; however, for simplicity's sake, in 2001 it began recognizing payments made by its long-standing customers as revenue when those payments were received. "It all evens out in the end," was Robyn's reply when you asked her about this change.

3. In reviewing the accounting for the bond issued to Mr. Barnsworth, you discovered that the effective interest rate for a bond of that type was 8% and that Mr. Barnsworth had paid a premium of $301,436. The journal entry made was as follows:

| Dr. Cash | (B/S) | 2,301,436 | |
| --- | --- | --- | --- |
| Cr. Misc. Income | (I/S) | | 301,436 |
| Cr. Bond payable | (B/S) | | 2,000,000 |

To record the issuing of a bond to Mr. Barnsworth.

4. As part of the new expansion, PPI leased some equipment on September 1, 2003. The annual lease payments are $150,000, to be paid *at the beginning of each year* for six years. The first payment was made on September 1, 2003. PPI will not obtain ownership of the equipment at the end of the lease term. The fair value of the equipment is $800,000. The economic life of the equipment is expected to be seven years. The interest rate implicit in the lease is 8% (the same as PPI's incremental borrowing rate). As it has always done with all leases, PPI only records lease expenses when the lease payments are made. Thus there is nothing on the balance sheet related to this lease, and $150,000 of expense was recorded on September 1, 2003.

5. While going through PPI's files you came across a file labelled "Grandpa's dividends." Inside was a legal document that seemed to grant a $400,000 dividend to the founder of the company. You asked about this and were told that a one-time dividend had been declared when the founder retired in 1999 (he was the only shareholder when the dividend was declared). The dividend was declared because it seemed that the founder would need some cash. However, plans changed and he never took the money out.

As such, no journal entry was made in 1999 to record the declaration of the dividend, and since then no entry has been made to reflect the agreement. The founder still owns shares of PPI.

## Required

Prepare the report for Mr. Barnsworth.

# HAIR ACCESSORIES INC.

## *Carl K.L. Ching*

Hair Accessories Inc. (HAI) is a retail store that specializes in hair accessories for teenage girls. Ms. Cashgrab started the company four years ago by renting a small retail space in a strip plaza in midtown. The company now has five stores in various shopping malls in different regions.

The retailing of hair accessories is highly competitive, with average selling prices pretty much determined by the market. As a result, a company's success depends heavily on the effectiveness of its cost control procedures. During the first two years of operations, the growth of HAI was rather stagnant. It was having difficulty controlling costs, and this had an adverse impact on its overall profit margins. So two years ago, Ms. Cashgrab decided to hire Mr. Cheap, an accountant with extensive experience in cost management. Since this hiring, HAI has grown tremendously as a result of the various cost-cutting measures introduced by Mr. Cheap.

Ms. Cashgrab is very happy with what Mr. Cheap has done for HAI and has decided to give him a hefty raise. As part of the new compensation package, he will be entitled to a bonus based on 10% of the company's net income, beginning with statements for the year ended April 30, 2004.

HAI's accountant has recently retired. Ms. Cashgrab has hired you to advise on appropriate accounting policies for the financial statements HAI should use for the year ended April 30, 2004. She has asked you to prepare a report on the appropriate treatment for the following items:

1. During the year, HAI started a "prepaid coupon program" whereby HAI customers can pay $90 to purchase $100 of cash coupons to be used at any HAI store. Once issued, the coupons are nonrefundable. They expire two years after the original purchase date.

2. HAI spent approximately $100,000 during the year advertising in a prestigious magazine. The $100,000 included the cost of designing and producing the ads. According to the store managers, more people have been coming into the stores since the ad campaign came out.

3. In January 2004, HAI became subject to litigation. A customer is seeking damages of $500,000, claiming that some of the materials used in the manufacture of hair accessories sold by HAI caused permanent damage to her hair's pigments. HAI believes the claim has no legal foundation and has not agreed to settle.

4. In March 2004, HAI completed the development of its website and began selling its hair accessories through the Internet. To stimulate sales, HAI initiated a "satisfaction guarantee program" whereby HAI would allow its Internet customers to return their

purchases one year after initial purchase date as long as the hair accessories were in their original condition. If returned, HAI will pay the invoice price back to customer plus interest at 2% per annum on the returned item.

## Required

Provide the report to Ms. Cashgrab.

# ASTRO MUSIC

## *V. Umashanker Trivedi*

Astro Music sells and rents out new and old musical instruments. It has been in business for the past 15 years. Natasha purchased the business from its previous owner, Olga, at the beginning of this year and incorporated it as Astro Music Inc., a private limited company. Astro Music has a very good local reputation; even so, it has not been very profitable during the past few years. Natasha attributes the lack of profit to Olga's advancing age, which has prevented her from managing the business effectively and exploiting all available business opportunities.

The purchase involved a lump sum initial payment of $300,000 as well as sharing of profits (described below). Since Natasha could not finance the entire lump sum of $300,000 on her own, she persuaded her friend, Anastasia, to become an equal investor in the business by contributing $150,000. The agreement was that Anastasia could pull out of the business at the end of the first year and receive her investment back at that time. If this happens, Natasha will have to go to a bank to obtain a loan to replace Anastasia's investment. Natasha would rather not do this, since it would mean cash outflows for interest payments, which she is presently not paying given that Anastasia is an equity participant in the business and not a creditor. Anastasia will continue as an equity participant in Astro Music Inc. only if at the end of year 1, based on the financial statements, it seems that the business will begin turning a profit.

## Issues

1. The purchase price for Astro that Natasha paid Olga consisted of a lump sum amount of $300,000 and a percentage of annual profits from ongoing business for the first three years on a sliding scale: 25% of profits for year 1, 15% for year 2, and 7½% for year 3. By ongoing business, both Natasha and Olga are referring to those business activities of Astro that were in existence at the time of purchase, not new lines of activities that Natasha might introduce later on. The purchase price was paid mainly for Astro's list of customers, for its local reputation, and for its inventory of instruments.

2. Astro Music stocks musical instruments that can be sold or rented. Rental periods for the musical instruments range from six months to two years. Musical instruments, including those being rented out, typically have indefinite lives as long as they are maintained properly. Manufacturers of the instruments and retail competitors have been offering promotions to spur sales, and Astro has been forced to reduce its selling prices and rental charges in order to remain competitive.

3. Up until now, half of Astro's rental customers have chosen to pay in full at the time of the rental agreement; the rest have chosen to pay on a monthly basis. Those who pay the rental fee in a lump sum are given a discount of 5%. Olga had few problems collecting monthly fees from her customers; typically only 5% of her receivables went bad.

Also, in 50% of the cases where receivables went bad, Astro was unable to recover the rented instruments.

4. In the past, all the instruments sold by Astro were made by major manufacturers. This year, Natasha signed an agreement with a Czech firm: it would manufacture instruments, which Astro would then sell under its own brand.

5. Astro decided to offer a two-year warranty on the instruments sold under its brand. Since returning defective instruments to the Czech manufacturer would be very costly, the manufacturer agreed to provide Astro with a discount of 50% on any instrument found to have major structural defects/problems, with such discounts to be adjusted against future purchases. If an instrument was defective and the warranty had not expired, Astro would exchange it. Astro would not have found it cost effective to have the defective instruments repaired for resale. So it decided to accumulate these returned defective instruments and sell them as scrap to an outside party whose business it is to salvage parts from defective instruments. The price received for the scrap would not be substantial.

6. Pursuant to its agreement, in the middle of the year Astro placed a substantial order for musical instruments from the Czech manufacturer. Unfortunately, before the year ended that firm declared bankruptcy and closed its business. By then, Astro had been able to sell only half the musical instruments it had purchased initially from the Czech maker. The other half remain in inventory as of year end.

7. In the past year there has been an influx of immigrants into the local community, replacing the older residents. This has had three results for Natasha: (1) there are many more customers; (2) most customers are new; and (3) most new customers choose to pay by the month.

Natasha, Olga, and Anastasia are very close friends and want only those accounting policies to be followed that will provide a fair reflection of the business — subject, of course, to any constraints that might be present. At the same time, they want to know how these policies will affect their various objectives. So they have come to you and asked you to:

(a) identify the various users of Astro's accounting information and their objectives;
(b) identify the various accounting issues facing Astro;
(c) state those accounting policies that would most fairly reflect the underlying economic situation for the various accounting issues identified by you (again, subject to any constraints that might be present); *and*
(d) state how these accounting policies would affect the various objectives of the different users identified by you in (b). They would also like you to explain why you have chosen these policies.

## Required

Prepare a report including all the information requested above.

# AURELIUS DEVELOPMENTS LIMITED

## K. Bewley

Aurelius Developments Limited (ADL) was incorporated 10 years ago. Its business involves buying farmland in the regions surrounding Toronto and holding it until development permits have been obtained and market conditions are favourable for the development of residential housing units. Once a property is ready for development, ADL contracts with a construction company, DZ Builders (DZB), to build the houses. ADL handles the sales promotions and marketing of the houses as they become ready for occupancy.

The president of ADL, Marcia Au, owns 51% of the ADL common shares. The remaining common shares are held by various relatives of Ms. Au. ADL also has financed its operation through bank mortgages on the land. In addition to taking the land as security on these mortgages, the bank has taken Ms. Au's personal investments as collateral for additional security. Ms. Au now wants to issue preferred shares in ADL to private investors and use the proceeds to pay back the bank mortgages. The plan is to make the preferred shares nonvoting and to pay a noncumulative 6% dividend. Ms. Au has found an investor group that is interested in purchasing the preferred shares, but that group wishes to see financial statements prepared in accordance with GAAP before investing.

Ms. Au has asked for your advice on preparing GAAP financial statements and on other financial matters relating to her business. Up until now ADL has only prepared unaudited financial statements, primarily for tax purposes. In discussions with Ms. Au, and from reviewing the most recent annual financial statements (for the year ended October 31, 2001), you learn the following:

1. ADL currently owns 16 tracts of undeveloped land ranging from 40 to 230 acres. Nine of the tracts have been leased to farmers, who are growing crops and using the land as pasture. Two of the tracts have been approved for development, and ADL has entered into a contract with DZB to start their development in 2002.
2. ADL has capitalized the purchase price of the land, legal fees relating to the purchase, and land transfer taxes. All other costs related to the properties, such as property taxes, earth-moving costs, and fees for architectural plans, have been expensed in order to maximize tax deductions.
3. ADL's net income has varied widely over the years, showing profits in years when housing developments are completed and sold, and losses in other years. Revenue is recognized when each house is sold. The average development takes about 18 months to complete from the time construction begins.
4. Five of ADL's tracts of land are located in an area that, as a result of environmental protests, has been identified as an environmentally sensitive area. The Ontario government has decreed that this area cannot be developed; however, it has agreed to swap ADL's five properties for properties of similar size and condition in a region where

development is permitted. The new properties are closer to a major city and are near existing highways and public transportation.

5. ADL provides some building materials to DZB at cost. In early 2001, ADL's purchasing manager purchased a large quantity of lumber as lumber prices were expected to rise significantly. This amounted to enough lumber to complete the framing for both the approved developments. However, lumber prices have since fallen, and DZB is unwilling to pay ADL's "cost" because it can now get lumber for less from other suppliers.

6. To date, ADL has completed five housing developments. The first development, completed in 1990, made use of a new type of vinyl siding in a variety of pastel shades. Over time this siding has begun to deteriorate and turn an unattractive brown. The current owners of these homes have organized and are threatening legal action against ADL and the construction company for using faulty materials. There is a government-sponsored insurance plan for new homes, but it will not cover this claim because the construction material is not becoming unsafe, it is just ugly. ADL's lawyers are taking a position similar to that of the insurance plan — that the wear and tear on the siding material is the homeowners' responsibility.

7. DZB recently approached Ms. Au to try to purchase one of the two tracts it is currently developing. DZB has offered to pay ADL's book value for the land; furthermore, it will give ADL a 20% share of the pretax profit on house sales when the development is sold.

## Required

1. Provide the advice requested by the president of ADL.
2. Instead of being an advisor to ADL, assume you are advising potential investors in the preferred shares. What aspects of the financial statements and the preferred shares would be important to consider, and what other information might be helpful for their decision?

# PIPER CITY PHARMACY

## *K. Bewley*

Piper City Pharmacy (PCP) commenced business about three months ago, with one store on the main street of a small town. The business is owned by Jennifer Chan, a pharmacist. She hopes to build up the volume of sales so that she can eventually sell the business to a large pharmacy chain. To finance sales growth, PCP needs to obtain additional funds in order to purchase more inventory and expand the types of inventory the store sells to include gifts, cosmetics, and other household items. Ms. Chan has approached you, the local banker, with a financial statement for the first two months of operations (to September 30, 2001). She tells you that the accounting methods used in it are tentative and are based on advice from a neighbour. You examine the financial statements and ask some questions, and learn the following:

1. Inventory is purchased from a large drug wholesaler. PCP is entitled to volume rebates for most of its purchases. These are calculated at the end of June of each year and paid 30 days later.
2. PCP has a five-year lease on the store. The monthly rent is renegotiated at the end of each year for the following year, but cannot be increased by more than 10% in any one year.
3. PCP paid $60,000 to decorate the store and add walls around the pharmacy counter. These costs are being amortized at 1% per month.
4. Ms. Chan receives a salary of $4,000 per month from the business.
5. Advertising materials related to the store opening were printed at a cost of $3,000. About half these materials have been distributed. The financial statements show an asset of $3,000 relating to this.
6. During its opening sale, PCP offered a 10% promotional discount on many items. The price reductions were charged to 'Opening costs' and are being amortized over 24 months.

Ms. Chan has asked you for advice on the appropriateness of the accounting principles for all parties but especially for lenders. She will be asking you for a loan as soon as the financial statements are finalized.

## Required

Provide the requested advice.

# BYTES'N THINGS

## Kevin Markle

Bytes'n Things Ltd. (BNT) was started by Guy Kishman in 1991 and has grown steadily over the past 13 years. BNT is based in a medium-sized town and sells and services computers. Until recently its market for both sales and service was strictly local. In June 2003, Mr. Kishman decided to take a big step and expand BNT nationwide. This would require money. The company obtained a very large loan from a bank and also issued shares to a private investor, Mr. D. Pockets. Mr. Kishman owns 60% of the shares, Mr. Pockets 40%. Mr. Pockets lives in another part of the country and does not want to play in active role in the company. Mr. Kishman will continue to run the operations.

Mr. Kishman has always prepared the financial statements of BNT solely for inclusion with the company's annual tax return. He has come to you because he is unsure how to account for some of the new transactions. He wonders whether he will need to change his current accounting methods in light of the changes this year. He asks you to recommend changes in accounting practices to factor in the new business structure.

After a discussion with Mr. Kishman and a review of the company's records, you have identified the following issues:

1. The company sells service contracts to customers. The contracts last for 12 months and are paid by the customer in 12 equal instalments at the end of each month. Each contract entitles the customer to unlimited service for equipment malfunctions throughout the year. For simplicity's sake, Mr. Kishman has always recorded the contract revenue when the cash is received.

2. For the purpose of expanding into other geographic areas, BNT hired a marketing consultant to develop a plan for increasing awareness of its products. BNT paid the consultant a flat fee of $300,000 for a plan covering 2003 to 2005. BNT began implementing the plan in 2003, and it appears to be working well.

3. Customers order computers from BNT by phone or over the Internet. BNT does not begin building the computer until the order is placed. Once it is built, the computer is shipped to the customer. The customer then has 30 days to pay. Mr. Kishman has always recorded the revenue on receipt of cash from the customer. He has always found this easier because approximately 4% of the customers never pay.

4. To accommodate the expansion, BNT had to heavily upgrade the computer hardware in its head office. The list price of the equipment purchased was $500,000, but Mr. Kishman was able to negotiate a price of $469,000. Taxes added $70,000 to the price, and delivery costs were $20,000. Installation of all the equipment cost $30,000, but after it was installed, Mr. Kishman realized that he had not planned the installation very well, and an additional $26,000 was spent to have the installation redone. BNT took out a three-year insurance policy against loss of or damage to the equipment and paid $36,000 up front for the coverage.

5. The expansion went well right from the beginning, and BNT made significant sales in several new markets. It has recorded all of the revenue related to these sales. The collection of these amounts (it made all the sales on credit) has been very slow. BNT has yet to book any bad debt expense because it is brand new in the markets and does not have a basis on which to make the estimate.

## Required

Prepare a report and recommendations for Mr. Kishman.

# VALHALLA INC.

## V. Umashanker Trivedi

Valhalla Inc. (VI) sells Hawaiian handicrafts in mainland North America. VI is a private limited company. Recently, however, it acquired 25% of the voting shares of Paradise Private Limited (PPL), paying $1 million, ⅔rds in cash and the rest with its shares. The $1 million paid for 25% of the $2.8 million of the net identifiable assets of PPL and for its share of the goodwill generated by PPL. VI financed a portion of this purchase by issuing to the public 800 five-year bonds valued at $1,000 each and sold at a discount of 10%. A related bond covenant requires VI to refrain from declaring dividends unless it can maintain a certain level of annual net earnings and a maximum debt-to-equity ratio of 1.2:1. PPL sells Caribbean handicrafts in mainland North America.

Mr. Nakamura is the manager of VI. VI pays him an annual salary of $200,000. In addition, he receives a bonus based on the net income of VI. PPL, in order to benefit from the managerial expertise of Mr. Nakamura, requested his services from VI. VI agreed to this request. Under the agreement between VI and PPL, the latter will reimburse the former for the time Mr. Nakamura spends on PPL's affairs at 1½ times Mr. Nakamura's wage rate. Mr. Nakamura spent 35% of his time looking after the affairs of PPL during this year. At the end of the year, the amount owed by PPL to VI consequent to obtaining his services is still due.

PPL has agreed to sell VI's inventory on consignment. VI has agreed to pay PPL a commission of 25% of net sales. During the year, VI delivered 10,000 Hawaiian canoe figurines of a new type, each costing $150. The associated transportation costs were $250,000. PPI has agreed to sell the consigned goods at a markup of 50% over the cost of $150 of each figurine. By year end, 60% of the goods consigned by VI were sold by PPL. However, 20% of such sales were returned by customers, who contended the figurines were defective. These defective goods were duly returned by PPL to VI, after payment of $40,000 in transportation costs. VI has asked PPL to deduct this cost before sending the sales proceeds to it. As of year end, PPL still has not remitted these sales proceeds to VI. VI thinks the returned figurines can be refurbished at $10 each and resold at $75 each. On its own, VI has sold 20,000 of these figurines at $200 each; it has 10,000 more of them in its warehouse as of the end of the year.

VI obtained a patent five years ago on a Hawaiian massager, after incurring research costs of $450,000 and a further $300,000 more on development costs to bring it to market. Costs related to obtaining the patent came to $150,000. The economic life of the patent was estimated as 10 years. At that time VI decided to write off these costs to be consistent with government tax requirements. This year, VI successfully defended its patent against a competitor who tried to copy VI's design. Associated legal costs were $250,000. The court also awarded VI $1,000,000 compensation for lost sales resulting from the patent infringement. As of the end of the year, the competitor has not paid the $1,000,000. Furthermore, the competitor has filed for bankruptcy, and it is estimated that VI will be able to collect only 50 cents on the dollar.

At VI, Mr. Nakamura has always focused on the business development side of things, and his knowledge of accounting is sketchy at best. So far VI had been maintaining books mainly to address tax requirements, with tax minimization as a big objective. Mr. Nakamura has been told that because VI is a public company, from this year onwards it will have to follow something called "the GAAP." Mr. Nakamura has no clue as to what this "GAAP" is. He has come to know that you have almost completed your introductory accounting course and are quite adept at GAAP. So he has approached you for advice on the accounting policies that VI must follow from now on.

## Required

Prepare a report to Mr. Nakamura outlining the policies you recommend. In your report also indicate to Mr. Nakamura how the changes in the accounting policies will affect the different users and their objectives.

# GLOBAL TELECOM LIMITED

## *Carl K.L. Ching*

Global Telcom Limited (GCOM) is a successful equipment and service provider specializing in networking solutions and equipment for hospitals and medical clinics. The company has a year end of April 30. Mr. Bill Techie founded the company five years ago and has held 100% of its shares since its inception.

GCOM has been growing at a lightning pace from the start. This has attracted a number of competitors, which are working hard to recruit GCOM staff and other qualified individuals in the market. Thus the company *must* work equally hard to recruit workers and hold on to them. GCOM still holds a competitive advantage; even so, Mr. Techie understands that it may lose that advantage as its competitors gain a better understanding of the industry. He can see the day coming when GCOM will require additional funds to invest in additional research and development to maintain its advantage.

During a lunch meeting with GCOM's banker, Ms. Line, Mr. Techie briefly discussed the possibility of obtaining a loan. Ms. Line told Mr. Techie that GCOM would be able to obtain a loan payable on demand at prime plus 2%. Also, as part of the bank's lending policy, financial statements would have to be submitted on an annual basis and a minimum debt-to-equity ratio of 3:1 would have to be maintained.

In the past, Mr. Techie has not been overly concerned about financial reporting. However, as the company is growing and will likely be seeking additional financing, he has hired you to recommend accounting policies for GCOM to adopt. Mr. Techie has told you not to worry about the debt-to-equity ratio, as he believes he can always change accounting policies to ensure that GCOM is in compliance with the bank's requirements.

From talking to Mr. Techie, you have been able to gather the following additional facts about GCOM:

1. In the previous fiscal year, GCOM incurred $300,000 to develop a monitoring system for its workers' PCs. This system is designed to enable the company to identify the amount of time its workforce spends on matters not related to work (e.g., surfing the Internet). Mr. Techie felt that this system would make his staff concentrate more efficiently on their tasks. While this system was being tested, the staff expressed a great deal of resentment; some threatened to quit the company if GCOM adopted it.
2. GCOM manufactures all the equipment it sells. For the past two years it has purchased most of its raw materials — computer chips, LCD displays, and so on — from the same supplier. To reward GCOM's loyalty, the supplier has agreed to give a volume rebate of 10% to GCOM if total purchase volume for the calendar year exceeds a certain threshold. Based on GCOM's purchase pattern over the past two years, the company is on pace to reach the volume threshold set by its supplier.
3. GCOM's business is divided into two main areas: selling networking equipment, and developing networking software for its clients.
4. With regard to equipment sales, all sales are made on account with payment terms of 90 days. Any time within these 90 days, GCOM's customers may return the

networking equipment for any reason. However, a restocking charge based on 20% of the original purchase price will be charged to the customer if it does return the product back to GCOM.

5. Regarding the development of networking software for its clients, GCOM's customers typically get billed when the software project has been completed. It takes 18 months on average to complete a networking software development project.

6. In the past year, in order to maintain its competitive advantage, GCOM has begun offering a three-year warranty on all its networking equipment. The warranty covers the cost of replacement parts as well as labour to repair the equipment. GCOM equipment has always been well known for its reliability and durability.

7. Two years ago, GCOM leased some networking equipment to Mad Cow Medical Centre ("Mad Cow") at $5,000 per month. The term of the lease is 60 months. In the past year, GCOM has introduced new, state-of-the-art networking equipment to the market. As a result, the net realizable value of the networking equipment leased to Mad Cow has been lowered to $50,000, although its net book value is $80,000.

8. Over the past five years, GCOM has been accounting for inventory on a cash basis — that is, all inventory production costs have been fully expensed as incurred. The company has always maintained a very low inventory balance. However, as a result of the company's expansion, that balance has increased significantly this year. From talking to Mr. Techie, you learn that labour and raw material costs have been rising over the past few years.

## Required

Prepare a report with the recommendations that Mr. Techie asked you to provide.

# HARMONIC HEALING PRIVATE INC.

## V. Umashanker Trivedi

Harmonic Healing Private Inc. (HHP) was incorporated to publicize and practise a new and alternative medical therapy called Harmonic Healing. The following events took place during the year:

1. On January 1, 2001, Mr. Richardson advanced a five-year loan of $500,000 to HHP when it was incorporated by Mrs. Norma, its owner. At the time of incorporation. Mrs. Norma contributed $500,000 as capital (in cash). The loan carries an interest rate of 10%, payable every six months on July 1 and January 1. HHP accounts for the interest as an expense when paid.

2. Premises required for carrying on the practice of Harmonic Healing were leased for two years for $10,000. Payments are due at the beginning of each month.

3. Revenues from the Harmonic Healing practice during the year were $300,000 (all received in cash). The related operating costs, which did not include the rent and interest costs noted above, were $200,000 (all paid in cash).

4. HHP paid $400,000 for a publicity blitz that included running ads on the radio and in local newspapers. HHP estimated that the publicity would provide benefits for at least the first four years. So it capitalized the $400,000 and is now proposing to amortize that amount over the four years.

5. HHP also sells the Harmonic Healer, a device people can purchase to continue the Harmonic Healing procedure at home. During the year, HHP sold 2,000 Harmonic Healers. Because a Harmonic Healer is expensive — $500 — HHP allows its customers to pay the amount in three instalments. At year end, $200,000 worth of instalments had yet to be received. HHP does not expect any of the receivables to go bad.

6. Mrs. Norma holds the patent for the Harmonic Healer. HHP has to pay a royalty of $100 to Mrs. Norma for each Harmonic Healer sold. Based on an agreement between HHP, Mrs. Norma, and a manufacturer, HHP purchases the Harmonic Healers in bulk from the manufacturer at $250 each. HHP purchased 5,000 Harmonic Healers during the year. The royalty owed to Mrs. Norma on the 2,000 Harmonic Healers sold remains unpaid at the end of the year. Nothing is due to the manufacturer at year end.

7. One of the customers of HHP who purchased a Harmonic Healer during the year alleged that he suffered an electric shock when the device malfunctioned. Consequently, he sued HHP seeking damages of $500,000 for the physical and mental trauma resulting from the shock. The court case has generated a lot of bad publicity for HHP. Fearing more of it, HHP settled the case out of court for $300,000 on January 20, 2002, crediting the "Cash" account and debiting the "Loss consequent to court case" account on that date.

The year end of HHP is December 31, 2001. The financial statements of HHP for 2001 were finalized on January 31, 2002. The tax rate applicable to 2001 is 30%, to future years 50%.

Mr. Richardson has come to you for advice. He wants you to evaluate HHP's accounting policies and comment on its financial situation.

## Required

Prepare a report to Mr. Richardson based on the evaluation Mr. Richardson requires. Make any assumptions that appear warranted; state these assumptions clearly in your report. You *need not* provide financial statements in your report.

# S&P ETC.

## V. Umashanker Trivedi

Ms. S and her brother's wife Ms. P have been separately selling fashion jewellery and gift items respectively in flea markets for the past few years. They finally decided to quit their regular jobs this year and merge their two businesses. So they jointly opened a jewellery shop called S&P Etc. this year. S&P is incorporated and is equally owned by Ms. S and Ms. P. Ms. S contributed her jewellery (current market value of $50,000) to the business for her 50% share; P introduced gift items with the same market value for her 50% share. The jewellery had originally cost Ms. S $20,000; the gift items had originally cost Ms. P $22,000. Details follow:

1. The jewellery includes both ethnic Chinese and popular fashion items, including some brand-name jewellery. Many of the gift items are made by Ms. P herself using raw materials purchased in bulk from various distributors. S&P entered into a three-year contract this year with a manufacturer in China to manufacture jewellery under the S&P brand. S&P has guaranteed that it will buy $300,000 worth of jewellery from the manufacturer over the three-year period.

2. Merchandise is typically sold for cash; however, on various occasions such as Chinese New Year and Christmas, S&P hosts events in various offices, during which it sells its wares for credit. Customers at these events are billed a month later.

3. S&P knows from past experience that most of its sales occur around holidays such as Valentine's Day and Christmas. So they plan to stock up on their wares to meet expected demand. Items not sold during the events may have to be sold at deep discount afterwards — often below cost. Suppliers must be paid within 30 days of the purchase.

4. S&P accepts returns within a month of the sale. Returned fashion jewellery is not resold. If the goods are returned because they have defects, S&P typically gives credit for the same against future purchases for goods made by the same manufacturer.

5. Ms. S and Ms. P are helped in their business by their large extended family.

6. S&P has entered into a lease agreement for two years. Ten percent of the total rent for the two years was paid in advance; the balance of the rent was paid monthly.

7. To attract publicity, S&P provides free fashion jewellery for the host of an ethnic TV program aired every Saturday, as well as gift items to decorate the set. S&P is acknowledged for the jewellery and gifts at the end of each program. The jewellery is not returned; however, the gift items are returned to S&P and replaced with new items for the next show.

8. To promote their brands, manufacturers as well as local jewellers — including S&P — often jointly sponsor local events such as fashion shows and beauty contests. The manufacturers bear 60% of the costs; the other participants, including S&P, bear the remaining 40%.

9. There is an on-site jeweller at S&P, Mr. X, who does repairs or manufactures custom jewellery according to the customers' specifications. S&P requires a 30% nonrefundable advance for custom orders.

10. S&P has entered into contracts to distribute its wares on credit to 10 other jewellery shops outside the city. S&P will be paid cost plus a percentage of the selling price only if the jewellery is sold. Unsold jewellery will be returned to S&P at its cost.
11. S&P has a line of credit with the local bank, secured by all of S&P's assets. In addition, Ms. S and Ms. P have given personal guarantees for the line of credit.

## Required

Write a report to S&P that includes your advice to them on appropriate accounting policies to follow and records to maintain.

# SPARKLING JEWELLERS INC.

## V. Umashanker Trivedi

Mr. Ruby Goldman has been in the jewellery business for the past 30 years, operating his solely owned business, Sparkling Jewellers. This year he incorporated his business as Sparkling Jewellers (SJ) Inc. as part of his plan to sell the business and retire. SJ represents the major asset of Mr. Goldman, who expects the proceeds from transferring his business to the newly incorporated business to fund his retirement. His only daughter, Crystal Goldman-Silver, is the manager of the new company. The following additional information is provided regarding the transfer of the business to the new company:

1. The assets that were transferred to the new company are estimated to have a value of $2.5 million, consisting of the following: an inventory of precious stones with an estimated market value of $2 million; the store premises, estimated to be worth $500,000; and goodwill developed over the past 30 years, valued at $500,000. A bank credit facility of $500,000 is outstanding. The credit facility carries an interest rate of 9%.
2. The inventory of precious stones serves as collateral for the bank loan.
3. At the time of incorporation the building was estimated to have a useful life of 20 more years. However, in the past the store premise was depreciated using straight-line amortization over an estimated life of 25 years. At the time of transfer to the new company, the building had been depreciated for 10 years.
4. Mr. Ruby and his daughter Crystal each own 50% of the shares of the new company. The agreement between the company and its two shareholders requires the company to declare each year a cash dividend equal to 20% of net income after taxes.
5. Ms. Crystal paid $1 million in cash to Mr. Ruby for her 50% share in the new company.
6. Ms. Crystal, besides a salary, is entitled to a bonus based on net income before taxes.
7. Many jewellery manufacturers vie with one another to get shelf space in SJ, given its local popularity and high reputation. So SJ demands and obtains a flat up-front stocking fee from these manufacturers to carry their products for three years. Before incorporation, SJ used to treat the entire fee as income in the year received.
8. Over the years, Mr. Ruby has found that jewellery designed by up-and-coming jewellers often becomes very popular. Carrying inventories of such jewellery has been a big factor in SJ's success. So to encourage these young and upcoming jewellery designers, Mr. Ruby in the past has often agreed to stock their jewellery and allowed them to pay the stocking fee at any time within the three-year contract period. Mr. Ruby has also paid the entire purchase price of the jewellery up front. Often these jewellers have not gained popularity and have gone bankrupt and thus have ended up not paying the stocking fee. In these cases the inventory from these jewellers has become almost worthless. Ms. Crystal intends to continue this practice of encouraging up-and-coming jewellers by allowing them to defer their payments of stocking fees and by paying them up front for their wares.

9. To expand the business and to make better use of SJ's inventory of precious stones, Crystal has entered into sale agreements with other local jewellers. Under these agreements, SJ sells its precious stones to these jewellers; however, it is liable to buy back unsold precious stones at the end of 12 months at 125% of the original sales price. These repurchased precious stones can be resold at their original sale price.

## Required

Advise SJ Inc. about appropriate accounting policies and accounting records to adopt in relation to the incorporation of the new company and the new company's jewellery operations.

# CRYSTAL CUSTOM BUILDERS

## V. Umashanker Trivedi

Crystal Custom Builders (CCB) was incorporated this year with Mr. and Mrs. Tao as the sole shareholders, each holding 50% of the shares. Mr. Tao has been in the construction business for the past 20 years, building custom luxury homes ($750,000 and above) for the past 10 as a sole proprietor. Mrs. Tao looks after all the administrative duties relating to the business; Mr. Tao looks after the construction and various technical details. Their daughter Joan has been assisting them for the past five years. They expect her to eventually take over management of CCB. Further details follow:

1. Mr. Tao provided cash for his 50% share of the company. CCB purchased three pickup trucks and other building equipment with most of this cash. Mrs. Tao provided three different pieces of land with a total market value of $1,000,000 at the time of incorporating CCB for her 50% share. These pieces of land were purchased five years ago for $300,000.

2. CCB sees itself using the land in one or more of the following ways: (1) contract with customers to build homes on portions of these pieces of land; or, (2) first build homes and then sell the finished homes; or (3) sell the appreciated land as is without any construction.

3. CCB has contracts with its suppliers for purchasing various building materials such as cement, bricks, and lumber. CCH obtains bulk discounts of between 10% and 20% of the purchase price from its suppliers. CCB also gets two months' credit from its suppliers for its purchases.

4. CCB contracts with various local tradespeople — carpenters, electricians, and so on — to work on projects. All required materials are supplied by CCB's suppliers. Tradespeople are paid for their labour at contracted prices. Contracts are typically for a year. CCB pays its tradespeople on completion of work on a particular home.

5. Typically, a home takes eight months to two years to complete.

6. Prices for the custom homes are fixed at the time of signing the contract with the purchaser. CCB has to absorb any future increases in costs of materials, labour, and so on. Payment terms are as follows: 10% of purchase price at the time of signing the contract; an additional 20% two months later; and the remaining 70% when the house is delivered to the purchaser.

7. CCB provides the following warranties on its homes: one year comprehensive, two years for major problems, and seven years for structural problems. Disputes are decided by binding arbitration. There have not been many problems in the past (prior to incorporation).

8. CCB expects to incur various other costs. Examples: architect fees for generic house plans that can be used as a basis for customization; licence fees to be paid to the local municipality for zoning; and fees paid to engineers for site plans and to verify the structural soundness of house plans.

9. CCB has two site supervisors and four other employees. Each supervisor is in charge of more than one site (each site can have many homes under construction). The four building employees carry out miscellaneous repair jobs covered under warranty. Repairs relating to work done by the tradespeople are the responsibility of the tradespeople concerned. The four employees are paid straight salaries; the two site supervisors, besides salaries, are paid bonuses based on the overall profitability of CCB.

10. One of the built homes serves as a model home and sales office, which is manned by Mrs. Tao.

11. CCB has a line of credit with one of the major banks. The land, built homes, trucks, and equipment all serve as collateral for the line of credit.

## Required

Write a report to CCB that includes your advice to the Taos on appropriate accounting policies for them to follow and records for them to maintain.

# PREDATOR PRIVATE CORP.

## *Prem M. Lobo and V. Umashanker Trivedi*

Predator Private Corp. (PPC) buys businesses that it thinks are undervalued, develops them, and then resells them after a few years to others for a profit. PPC purchased the Nic-Naks brand division and associated assets from Down-At-The-Heel Corp. (DATH) five years ago. Mr. Smooth Operator, the majority shareholder and manager of PPC, is planning to sell the Nic-Naks Brand and wants to estimate its value. He has retained Mr. Straight N. Narrow, a consultant, to provide PPC with information on the fair market value (FMV) of the various assets purchased.

1. Mr. Narrow estimates that the fair market value of all assets at the time of purchase was $1 million. PPC had paid $1 million for the assets, consisting of $750,000 in cash and the rest in shares of Predator Private Corp.
2. Mr. Narrow estimated that the land and building purchased had an FMV of $250,000 ($50,000 land and $200,000 building) at the time of purchase, and the building had an estimated useful life of 20 years. However, Smooth contended that real estate prices were temporarily depressed at the time of purchase; according to him the correct values of the land and building were $50,000 and $300,000. So Smooth went ahead and accounted for the land and building at those values in PPC's books. Furthermore, Smooth felt that under his brilliant management, exceptional repairs and maintenance of the building would be undertaken. Therefore, its estimated useful life would be 30 years.
3. Mr. Narrow estimated that the machinery purchased had an FMV of $100,000 with an estimated useful life of 5 years. He also indicated that the machinery should be depreciated using the double declining balance method, given the high likelihood that the machinery would become obsolete by then because of advances in technology. Again, Smooth disagreed, contending that the market prices were temporarily depressed, and recorded the machinery at its "correct" value of $200,000, and estimated its useful life at 10 years. Furthermore, he also decided that under his careful care the machinery would provide PPC with the same amount of benefit over all the 10 years and decided to use the straight-line amortization method.
4. Mr. Narrow thought that the inventory purchased was worth $250,000 and that LIFO would be the most suitable cost-flow measure. However, Smooth readily recognized that the tax authority does not recognize LIFO and chose to use the FIFO cost-flow method. Furthermore, Smooth conceded that despite his managerial ability he may have overpaid for the inventory, and chose to allocate only $150,000 as the cost of inventory. He also stated that he was satisfied that this mistake on his part was more than made up by his "superior" purchase decisions regarding the building and the machinery above.
5. The balance of the purchase price constituted goodwill. Mr. Narrow felt that the benefits of the purchased goodwill were uncertain and suggested that it be amortized over 5 years. Smooth thought that Narrow was very conservative and vaguely remembered from the one accounting class he took in school that goodwill has indeterminate life.

Therefore, he decided not to amortize goodwill. Furthermore, he contended that PPC was building significant amount of goodwill under his capable leadership. So he increased the balance in the goodwill account by $10,000 each year by debiting the goodwill account and crediting net income by that amount.

6. The business of Nic-Naks requires constant innovation. Therefore, PPC incurred significant amounts of research and development expenses. This year these costs amounted to $75,000. Smooth chose to capitalize these costs, contending that they create intangible assets for PPC. Moreover, Smooth chose not to amortize capitalized research and development (which totals, including this year's costs, to $450,000) because of his view that these expenses generate revenues for the company for many years into the future.

7. Smooth, being the manager of PPC in addition to being a majority owner, receives a straight salary every month. In addition, Smooth also earns an annual bonus based on the annual net income of PPC.

8. At the end of five years, PPC decided to sell off the Nic-Naks Brand and approached Mr. Gullible with an offer to sell the company to him. Mr. Gullible and Smooth have tentatively agreed that the selling price will be a multiple of five times the current year's net income. This is consistent with multiples used to value similar businesses in the industry. Net income for the Nic-Nak division for the current year is reported as $500,000 per the 2002 financial statements.

9. PPC has provided Mr. Gullible with the financial statements relating to the Nic-Naks Brand for the past five years. Mr. Gullible is not sure of what to make of these financial statements. So he has turned to you for advice.

## Required

Prepare a report to Mr. Gullible analyzing the information provided above and critically assessing the accounting policies chosen by PPC. Discuss the impact of the chosen accounting policies and identify any issues that Mr. Gullible should be concerned about.

# LAKE BELOVED

## V. Umashanker Trivedi

Kabir is a wellness instructor with 10 years' experience teaching yoga and fitness. He is excited about an investment opportunity: a 100 acre property, mostly wooded, known as Lake Beloved. There are two buildings on the property, which is 70 kilometres northeast of the city in cottage country. One of the buildings is presently being used as a diner; the other is an abandoned hotel. Kabir sees a golden opportunity to develop a spa and retreat. He immediately discusses the investment opportunity with his childhood friend, Walter. Walter is now just as excited and has agreed to loan Kabir half the purchase price at 10%. Further details:

1. The current owner is demanding $1 million for the property. She believes that 70% of the value of the property is in the diner, 20% in the unused building, and 10% in the land. Kabir believes otherwise. In his view, 70% of the value is in the abandoned building, 20% in the diner, and 10% in the land.

2. In the long run the surrounding land could turn out to be the most valuable part of the property. Land values in the district have been rising now that families are beginning to use their cottages as permanent residences to escape the overcrowded city. This means that the land belonging to Lake Beloved could appreciate considerably if it is rezoned for housing. However, the land may never be rezoned, given that environmentalists are strongly opposed to further development in the district and are winning this battle.

3. The current owner is willing to continue running the diner if she gets to keep 75% of the net income from it; Kabir would get the remaining 25%.

4. Kabir estimates that it will take him another $300,000 to convert the abandoned hotel into a wellness/fitness centre.

5. Kabir believes he can charge $200 per person per day for the facilities of the wellness centre.

6. Kabir intends to enter into agreements with corporations in the city allowing their employees access to the centre's facilities. Under the agreement each corporation will pay a minimum flat fee of $100,000, which will allow it 1,000 person days of access to the wellness centre (i.e., at an average discounted rate of $100 per person per day). Any use exceeding the 1,000 person-days will be charged to the corporation at the usual rate of $200 per person per day.

7. To encourage patrons to pay the regular $200 rate, Kabir wants to institute a rewards program whereby each day's stay will earn them 100 wellness points. These wellness points will have to be redeemed within three years of being earned. Wellness points can be used to pay for a stay or for purchases made at the on-site boutique, which will sell herbal wellness products and related items. One hundred wellness points will equal $10; thus, 2,000 wellness points will be needed to pay for a day's stay at the regular $200 rate.

8. Kabir intends to join an association of wellness centres across North America. To promote the use of one another's facilities, the wellness points earned by customers at any member centre are redeemable at the facilities of other centres at the rate of 100 wellness points equals $5. Under the agreement, individual facilities must settle in cash the balance of wellness points earned/owed to one another at the end of each calendar year.

9. Kabir intends to reach an understanding with local tour companies whereby Lake Beloved will recommend these tour companies to its customers for local sightseeing; in turn they will promote Lake Beloved to their customers. No exchange of money is proposed.

10. The local municipality charges municipal taxes on local businesses at 2% of net income.

Kabir and Walter want to investigate the investment opportunity further. To this end, they want to analyze projected financial statements, including an income statement, a balance sheet, and a cash flow statement, for the first ten years for Lake Beloved. They have come to you for suggestions regarding suitable accounting policies and procedures to account for the purchase and subsequent operations of Lake Beloved while preparing these projected financial statements. Kabir wants to incorporate the new business as a private company. The loan by Walter will be to the company, not to Kabir. Kabir has $450,000 of his own money, with which he intends to help capitalize the business. The rest will be funded by a bank loan to the company.

## Required

Prepare a report to Kabir and Walter advising them about the appropriate accounting policies and procedures to follow when they prepare the projected financial statements relating to the proposed investment both at the time of acquiring it and while operating it during the first 10 years.

# PRINTTALK INC.

## *Kevin Markle*

Printtalk Inc. (PI) is a private company owned by three shareholders. Joel Collins owns 55% of the common shares, Karen Rivas 35%, and Scott Dixon 10%. Dixon also holds a convertible bond from PI that allows him to convert the bond into additional common shares (at his option) if a specified target of owners' equity is met on the October 31, 2005, financial statements of PI. If the conversion is made, the percentages of ownerships would change to Collins 36%, Rivas 24%, Dixon 40%.

The company has a profit-sharing plan for senior managers whereby they receive additional compensation of 15% of reported net income each year. The three owners also wish to receive dividends of approximately 50% of net income each year. The company is partially financed with a line of credit from a major bank. The maximum amount of the line of credit is determined by the collateral value of PI's net assets.

Because there are a variety of users with differing needs, the board of directors of PI decided that accounting should be done in accordance with GAAP unless doing so yields information that is less useful or accurate than information provided by a method which departs from GAAP. The accounting records of PI are to be maintained by Collins. However, the other shareholders have a right of access to the accounting records. If they disagree with a decision that has been made, they can request that an independent arbitrator be brought in to settle the dispute. All decisions of the arbitrator are binding on all parties.

PI commenced operations on November 1, 2002, and has an October 31 year end. Collins prepared the financial statements for the first year ended October 31, 2003. The shareholders could not agree on the financial statements. After much discussion, the owners decided to send their disputes about the first year's statements to the arbitration process.

It is now December 2003. You are employed by Arbigreat, the arbitration company hired by PI to resolve the issues. You have been asked to review all matters that are in dispute and provide a draft report to John Smith, a retired judge employed by Arbigreat, who will render the binding decisions. Smith wants a full report from you, giving a complete analysis of each disputed matter, with supporting reasoning for your conclusions.

You have made several inquiries and have learned that PI has developed technology to transcribe voice into print at an economical cost. The technology has been well received in venues such as courts and legislatures. PI sells software and also conducts special consulting assignments and long-term contracts for clients. To maintain its competitive edge, PI has to engage in constant R&D. Some research is merely to improve the existing popular software; however, significant funds are also spent developing new products.

All of those who have reviewed the financial statements (Rivas, Dixon, the managers, and the bank) have expressed some concerns. You have been able to gather the following additional information directly from the complainants:

1. The convertible bond that Dixon holds was issued on November 1, 2002. It has a face value of $500,000, a maturity date of October 31, 2012, and a coupon rate of 6%. The

effective rate for that kind of bond on November 1, 2002, was 7%. The effective rate for that kind of bond on October 31, 2003, was 5%. The amount showing on the balance sheet of PI for fiscal 2003 is $500,000, and the interest expense included on the income statement is $30,000.

2. The job market for top software engineering talent is very tight. As a result, PI has turned to information technology "head hunters" to attract key personnel from other high-tech companies. During the year, PI paid $178,000 in placement fees, which were expensed as salary costs. The search firm offers a one-year money-back guarantee if any of the people hired leave the company or prove to be unsatisfactory.

3. For cash flow purposes, PI leases all of its computer and office equipment. The lease calls for annual payments of $300,000 at the end of each year for the next eight years (through 2010). The interest rate implied in the lease is 8%. PI has agreed to buy all of the equipment for $1 at the end of the lease. Only the October 2003 payment of $300,000 has been expensed.

4. PI got its product to market just months ahead of a competitor. The competitor has launched a patent infringement lawsuit against PI alleging that PI used part of the competitor's program. The lawsuit is for $2,000,000. It is not expected to go to trial for at least two years. Collins expensed the entire $2,000,000 and recorded a liability when he found out that one of the competitor's key programmers had been hired by PI early in this fiscal year. Legal counsel feels that PI has a good chance of defeating the charges, but has suggested that it may be more economical to offer a settlement amount of $900,000 in order to avoid any bad publicity that could arise once the lawsuit is made public.

## Required

Prepare the report for John Smith.

# HARLEY INC.

## V. Umashanker Trivedi

Harley, a private limited company, has since its inception 10 years ago developed a reputation as a supplier of top-quality school uniforms. The head office and manufacturing facilities are in Toronto, with a branch in Mississauga. Harley owns the buildings and structures housing these facilities. All these facilities have zero book value, having been fully depreciated. One-quarter of the main office building has been given rent-free to a local charity supported by Harley.

Harley takes pride in supporting the Canadian economy by choosing Canadian manufacturers. It also uses only reputable, ethical companies with proven expertise in school apparel to make most of its garments (the remainder being manufactured in its own facility). Harley stands behind all its garments. It provides personalized service and 100% customer satisfaction. All mandatory uniform items are guaranteed to provide normal wear for one school year.

Some schools choose unique uniform designs; others merely need their logo embroidered on stock uniforms. Consequently, Harley has to maintain designs that can be sold only to students of specific schools, as well as uniforms that can quickly be customized for a particular school (by embroidering a logo). Schools have the right to change their uniform colours for a new academic year; however, not every school changes its uniform colour every year.

Harley encounters different types of up-front costs in relation to its bids to get exclusive supplier rights to different schools. Specifically, as part of the bidding process it has to come up with 'prototype' uniforms to show to school authorities. This exercise is expensive, since Harley has to contract the design process to costly apparel designers. Furthermore, significant commissions are paid to Harley's salespeople for bids won. In addition, these salespeople earn commissions based on sales generated from bids won by them. Harley does not win every bid. Exclusive supplier contracts, when won, are for periods of three to five years. However, schools do not provide guarantees about the minimum number of uniforms that will be purchased by the students. Instead, schools typically provide Harley with the number of students enrolled with them at different levels so that Harley can plan their inventory levels.

While most of the work is contracted out, Harley also has machinery to fill rush orders. Some of the machinery is school specific (i.e., a particular machine purchased for manufacturing the uniforms for one school will not be useful for manufacturing the uniforms for another school). Manufacturing apparel in-house, compared to contracting out work, is costly and time consuming; also, Harley's managers must devote more of their time to the process. To encourage investment in capital goods, the Canadian government provides a tax credit of 25% of the cost of machinery.

During the year, Harley discovered that one of its contractors, instead of manufacturing all the apparel in Canada, was having a portion manufactured in a Third World country and then shipped to Canada. Furthermore, this contractor had been found guilty of disposing of fabric waste illegally in Canada. Harley immediately terminated the agreement with that contractor. However, this has adversely affected Harley's reputation. In addition, it has created a shortage of uniforms, and some orders are going unfilled. As a result, various lawsuits have been filed against Harley both by the concerned school authorities and by some individual parents. Harley in turn has sued its contractor. The contractor has filed for bankruptcy, but Harley believes it can recover 70% of its lawsuit-related costs from the ex-contractor. Nothing has been resolved as of year end. Harley also has had to pay a fine of $100,000 to the government in relation to the illegal dumping of the fabric waste, since it has been held partially liable for that act. Harley is not sure whether this amount can be recovered from its ex-contractor.

At the beginning of the current fiscal year, intending to expand its operations, Harley acquired a 30% interest in Davidson, another private limited company, which makes safety apparel for industrial use and which has a single store in Hamilton. Davidson has not been doing that well lately. Under the agreement between Harley and Davidson, the former will provide the latter with management advice. Also, Harley will get to place one of its managers on Davidson's board of directors. The agreement requires Davidson to pay 10% of its net income before taxes as a management fee to Harley. Harley has issued common shares valued at $1 million to the Davidson family for its 30% stake in Davidson; that is $200,000 above the fair market value of the net assets of Davidson. The Davidson family continues to own the remaining 70%. The $1 million worth of shares give the Davidson family a 10% shareholding in Harley. Harley has also paid the Davidson family $100,000 for the right to purchase, at its option, the remaining 70% of the shares in Davidson at any time in the next two years. The purchase would be at the fair market price at that time as determined by an outside consultant. Harley will forfeit the $100,000 if it chooses not to purchase the remaining 70%.

Davidson, under the management advice of Harley, made a profit of $250,000 before calculating the management fee and income taxes in the current year (Harley's year end is May 31, while that of Davidson is June 15). Davidson declared and paid $100,000 as a dividend to its shareholders at year end. However, given the current controversy surrounding Harley, both companies have decided to part ways. Harley has relinquished its 30% holding in Davidson by receiving back its shares issued to the Davidson family and paying them an additional $227,500 in cash on June 30. Harley procured this cash through a bank loan, using its machinery and office and manufacturing facilities as collateral.

It is now June 30. Until this year, Harley's managers did not spend much thought on the accounting aspect of its business. Given the various changes it has experienced this year, Harley has approached you for advice on appropriate accounting policies. Assume that the tax rate applicable to both companies is 20%.

## Required

Prepare a report outlining your recommendations to Harley's management. Show all necessary calculations.

# INTERMEDIATE CASES

As you use the cases in this book, your familiarity and comfort level with case analyses will increase. You will be able to handle more complex cases by applying the same processes as you have used with simpler cases. The cases in Chapter 7 and Chapter 8 of this book provide additional challenges to your case analysis skills. These cases have been classified as "intermediate" for one of three reasons. First, some cases use concepts that you may not have been exposed to until a few weeks into an introductory accounting course. This will depend on how your instructor has organized the course and the order in which topics have been presented — so don't be surprised if your instructor uses an "intermediate" case early in the course. Second, some cases are simply longer. With more textual material to read and process, you will need to apply your case analysis techniques more systematically. This will be easier to do if you have practised your skills on more straightforward cases first. Finally, some cases are short but capture issues that have many levels of implications. We have classified these as "intermediate" or "advanced" to signal and recognize that these cases may deal with issues on which professional accountants and standard setters have yet to reach a consensus. These are rich cases that should stimulate debate about how transactions should be reported.

# TAMPICO AIRWAYS

## *Arthur R. Guimaraes*

Tampico Airways (Tampico) is a regional airline operating to coastal cities on the Gulf of Mexico. Tampico is a private company owned 100% by Mr. Perez and was established only six months ago. Mr. Perez has hired a manager, Mr. Guimas. Mr. Guimas has experience in the airline industry and will be responsible for all aspects of the business, including financial accounting. His pay will be based largely on his ability to meet certain profit targets.

Mr. Perez was instrumental in starting the business, and contributed $500,000 of his own money, but he is not familiar with financial accounting and thus has consummated some transactions without considering the accounting implications.

The following issues have arisen:

1. Tampico purchased two brand-new planes when Mr. Perez started the airline. Each has fifty seats and cost $4 million and was financed in part by a local bank, Bancormex.
2. Mr. Guimas has received a stock option of 1,000 shares at $5 each. A valuation of Tampico when the options were granted established a per share value of $10.
3. Tampico spent $800,000 on an advertising campaign. Mr. Perez insists that the money was well spent, as it will lead to future sales and the establishment of the Tampico brand name.
4. On Tampico's maiden flight, a passenger slipped on a banana peel while boarding and broke her leg. It was established that a cabin attendant had dropped the peel there. The lawsuit is for $500,000. Mr. Perez estimates that he can settle for $200,000.
5. Tampico sells tickets up to one year in advance of the flight. Tickets are nonrefundable; however, changes can be made for a fee of $150. Approximately 25% of tickets purchased are later changed and subject to the fee of $150.

Mr. Perez has provided the following forecast:

- Expected ticket sales of 25,000 per year
- Average ticket price of $700
- Seat occupancy rate of 90%

Mr. Perez is considering adding an Air Miles program and would like to know what the implications for accounting would be.

Mr. Perez has come to you for advice on accounting issues, as it is approaching year end, December 31. He would like to review the financial statements in a few weeks.

## Required

Prepare the memo to Mr. Perez.

# AIR DE ROSE

## *Alan T. Mak*

Francesco De Rose is the president of Air De Rose (ADR), a regional discount carrier based in Toronto. The common and preferred shares are held by the De Rose family. ADR has also raised capital by issuing corporate debt, which is traded on the Toronto Stock Exchange. At the time, debt financing seemed ideal because of the tax deductibility of interest and because it enabled the De Rose family to retain control of ADR.

ADR's profits have been declining steadily over the past year. Fuel prices have increased over 100% in the past 12 months. Francesco had believed that fuel prices would remain stable or even fall due to the slowing economy. Thus he did not follow the usual ADR policy of purchasing forward contracts for jet fuel. ADR has been forced to purchase fuel at the prevailing (higher) spot rate in the open market. Another factor affecting profitability is intense price competition from the larger national carriers. Air Canadian has been offering deep-discount fares for the same routes serviced by ADR. As a result of rising costs and falling revenues, ADR has been finding it difficult to meet its payment obligations.

Yankee Airlines (YA) is major competitor based in Chicago. YA has been trying to expand into the Canadian market but has been unsuccessful securing additional routes under the Open Skies Agreement. ADR seems like an ideal opportunity to break into the Canadian market. YA is considering making an equity investment in ADR and has asked for a financial report "appropriate for our purposes."

Francesco understands that ADR's financial statements have long been prepared with the objective of minimizing tax liabilities. As far as he is concerned, "numbers are numbers," and he doesn't know what YA is expecting from this report. He has asked you, the CFO, what this special-purpose report for ADR should include and how it might be different from ADR's normal financial statements.

In the course of your research, you have identified the following facts:

1. Passengers typically book through ticketing agents or directly with ADR through its website. Tickets may be put "on hold," with no deposit required. The customer may confirm and order on-hold tickets any time during the seven-day holding period. The on-hold program was made available for potential passengers who were shopping around for prices. Once tickets are ordered, payment is required in cash or by major credit card. Full-price tickets may be refunded in full if the passenger does not make the flight. Discount tickets are given credit against future flights. ADR currently recognizes revenue once the flight is completed.
2. ADR is a participant in FreeFlight, a frequent flyer program sponsored by a number of regional airlines. Typically, 10% of the passengers on each ADR flight are flying "free" from the FreeFlight program. As income tax law prescribes, ADR expenses the costs of the FreeFlight program as they are incurred (paid).
3. Emilio Lagazi, a childhood friend of Francesco, is the supplier of ADR's in-flight meal service. Emilio has given ADR a significant discount to "help out" ADR. ADR has recorded the amount charged/paid for the meal service in its accounts.

4. Many members of Francesco's family work for ADR. They are involved in every level of the business, from senior manager to flight attendant to ticket agent. Given the amount of time and effort they devote to the business, Francesco has been taking care of all their living expenses. ADR pays for housing, meals, and even clothing expenses for all family members. These amounts are expensed as part of salary costs.

5. ADR has developed a proprietary online reservation system. This system is used for all ADR bookings and is also licensed to other regional competitors for their bookings. The software is compatible with all reservation systems currently used by the airline industry, and its popularity is growing wildly. Francesco believes that the $5 million the system cost was money well spent, because of the synergies an industrywide reservation system could generate. For financial accounting purposes, the R&D costs for this system were expensed as the costs were incurred.

## Required

Prepare your report to Francesco.

# BALLI CONTRACTING LIMITED

## A. Scilipoti

Joe Balli is the 100% owner of Balli Contracting Ltd. (BCL), a private Canadian company. BCL has just entered into a contract with a small South African company to build a new condominium complex near the Air Canada Centre in Toronto. BCL specializes in building large industrial and commercial buildings; this is its first contract to construct a residential building. To finance construction of the complex, BCL entered into a financing arrangement with a bank for $3 million. The bank has requested audited financial statements prepared according to GAAP.

The contract price is $4.5 million. The complex must be completed in three years. BCL has determined that the total cost of the building will be $3.3 million. Joe has obtained the services of one of the largest condo builders in Toronto to help him price the job. He expects that the building will be completed in over three years.

The costs are expected to be incurred as follows: $1.6 million in year 1; $1 million in year 2; and $0.7 million in year 3. BCL will receive progress payments of $1 million in year 1 and $1.5 million in year 2; the balance will be paid only when the building has a 75% occupancy rate — that is, when the building is 75% sold. BCL has also agreed to absorb all repair costs to the building up to 365 days after the completion date.

## Required

1. Discuss alternative revenue recognition policies that BCL could use for the condominium project, and recommend an appropriate method.
2. (Optional) Provide the related journal entries for the three years in accordance with your recommended policy.

## BAND ON THE RUN

### A. Scilipoti

On returning home from a busy day at school, you receive a telephone call from an old high school friend, Oliver. After gossiping about which of your friends are married, in jail, and so on, Oliver begins to tell you about a great business idea.

Oliver, a struggling musician, has decided to start a business, Band On The Run (BOR). BOR will produce and distribute online concerts. Oliver and his band, The Lady Bugs, will perform concerts in Oliver's garage, which has recently been converted into a music studio. The concerts will be distributed in real time over the Internet to customers who "buy" concert tickets over the Internet.

After a long search, Oliver has found a company that has developed a technology that will facilitate the online transfer of the music and video at acceptable quality.

At this point, Oliver needs cash to purchase the computer hardware and software, buy outfits for himself and his band, and buy "digital ready" musical instruments, and as working capital. He has contacted you after remembering you have accounting expertise. He is unsure what the best method is to "get some cash to pay for all of this stuff, dude." He would like a detailed analysis from you of the options available to him, including concrete and supported recommendations. Furthermore, he needs to prepare financial statements and would therefore also like you to indicate which types of "accounting information" will be required for each of the alternatives you suggest and the impact each will have on the required "accounting information."

### Required

Prepare the report requested by Oliver.

# BEAUTY MANUFACTURING LIMITED

## A. Scilipoti

Beauty Manufacturing Limited (BML) is a manufacturer of video lottery terminals in Thunder Bay, Ontario. The company produces the most sophisticated lottery terminals in the world and sells the units primarily to Canada's provincial governments. Because the company has been growing rapidly, Ana Beauty, who owns 100% of the common shares of BML, has needed to find additional working capital wherever she can. Over the past year, ended September 30, 2000, BML has run through Ms. Beauty's initial investment of $175,000 in exchange for common shares, as well as a $200,000 bank loan. The bank has refused her additional financing beyond the $200,000 loan already given.

Recently she received an offer to purchase a 40% interest in the company from Mr. Mickey Mouse, a wealthy investor. Mr. Mouse has requested financial statements for the September 30, 2000, year end before making a final offer.

As a result of her poor cash position and a few family problems, Ms. Beauty has become delirious. She has limited knowledge of accounting and has asked you to assist her with BML's year end accounting.

You meet Ms. Beauty and learn the following:

1. An order for terminals worth $2.5 million will be shipped to Quebec in the fall of 2000; these machines will carry a two-year warranty against defective parts and workmanship. A deposit of $1,000,000 was received by BML in September 2000.
2. Equipment costing $480,000 was acquired on September 1, 2000, and recorded as a utility expense. The equipment has an expected useful life of 10 years and zero salvage value.
3. On August 1, 2000, BML purchased a one-year insurance policy for $240,000. Payment is due October 2, 2000.
4. Based on discussions with Bruno, the accounts receivable clerk, and Ms. Beauty, you learn that BML has been unable to collect $44,500 of accounts receivable. A $20,000 write-off is related to a customer that went bankrupt on October 5, 2000.
5. Ms. Beauty estimates that during the year ended September 30, 2000, the following costs were incurred by BML to obtain the order from Quebec:

| | |
|---|---:|
| Production time & material | $ 500,000 |
| Time of senior management | 250,000 |
| Time of marketing staff | 200,000 |
| Accounting staff salaries | 75,000 |
| Related travel costs | 150,000 |
| Donated time from Ms. Beauty's mother, who speaks French (estimated) | 100,000 |
| Total | $1,275,000 |

6. BML entered into a contract with its salespeople to pay them a bonus equal to 5% of BML's profits. BML generated $2,000,000 of sales in 2000, all of which were collected during the year. BML had cost of goods sold of $1,000,000, all of which were paid during the year. No bonus has been paid as of the year end.

7. BML received a $200,000 legal bill — which was fully paid as of September 30, 2000 — for services rendered during the year then ended. The bill was subdivided as follows:

   • $50,000 related to incorporation requirements.
   • $50,000 to register patents associated with the new Quebec lottery terminals.
   • $100,000 for work related to a divorce settlement between Ms. Beauty and her estranged husband Bill.

## Required

Bill, Ms. Beauty's now ex-husband, was the controller of BML until he was fired after a scandal involving Monica, the production manager. You have been hired to help Ms. Beauty prepare the September 30, 2000, year end financial statements.

1. Outline the users of the BML financial statements. Indicate each of their individual needs and financial reporting objectives. Which of the noted objectives of accounting should be followed, and why? Are there any constraints that should be followed? Explain why.

2. Prepare any required journal entries to record the transactions for fiscal 2000. Also, provide any adjusting entries as required. State all your necessary assumptions, and if necessary provide the original entries. Remember to tie back to your answers in 1.

3. Identify the financial statements for the year ended December 31, 2000, that you consider appropriate under the circumstances. Explain why they are appropriate.

# BLOOMING BEAUTY

## A. Scilipoti

Bob and Doug Goodman's grandfather began Blooming Beauty ("Beauty") in 1939. Papa Goodman immigrated to Niagara, Ontario, from Poland in 1938 and purchased 1,500 acres of farmland for a nominal dollar amount. Papa Goodman made Beauty famous for its fresh-cut flowers and small plants. He operated the business as a sole proprietorship until he died suddenly in 1999.

The twins Bob and Doug grew up in the business after an airplane crash killed their parents when they were very young. Beauty grows and sells flowers and small plants — wholesale only — to landscapers and large chain stores across Canada and the United States. Since Papa Goodman died, Bob and Doug have been running the operations.

Beauty was never incorporated because Papa Goodman never trusted anyone. As a sole proprietorship, the business grew very slowly over the years and was never extremely profitable. Yet the family never lacked cash, and Bob and Doug knew this. Bob and Doug have always dreamed of expanding the family operations by adding staff and acreage and selling their products direct to consumers on the Internet.

Last weekend, in a bar outside Toronto, you ran into Bob and Doug. They had already heard about your accounting expertise, and now they approach you asking for business advice. What organizational structure should Beauty use? What alternatives do they have to finance expansion? And would you help them select accounting policies for Beauty's December 31, 1999, year end financial statements?

You agree to help Bob and Doug. They explain that they will require a report that includes detailed support for your recommendations. After spending one week at the farm, you have compiled the following information.

1. Because cut flowers have a shelf life of roughly one week, they are cut only when orders are received. Beauty has always recorded revenue when cash is received from its customers because Papa never trusted anyone. The final invoiced sales price is adjusted for dead or damaged flowers and plants when Beauty's customers receive them. Papa always chose to wait until the very last minute to make adjustments for damages. Bob and Doug explain that the damages are never more than approximately 10% of shipments.
2. The 1,500 acres of land are being carried at the cost of $1,500. After researching, you learn that one acre of land adjacent to the Goodman property recently sold for $100,000. Bob and Doug are very excited because their grandfather gifted the farmland to them.

## Required

Prepare the report to Bob and Doug.

# POREL CORPORATION

## A. Scilipoti

Porel Corporation ("Porel") is a software development company that was incorporated in Canada in 1981. The company's two founding shareholders, Brian Matthews and Richard Chen, considered by some to be software geniuses, have always kept a close watch over the company's financial situation.

The company operates in the highly competitive office-productivity software industry. Porel's main product, LetterPerfect Suite, is a fully integrated software package that includes word processing and spreadsheet management components as well as a desktop presentation program. Porel's main competitor, MacroHard Corporation, has a 95% share of the office-productivity software market thanks to its highly successful MacroHard Office package.

In spite of the market's fierce competition, Porel has managed to maintain its market presence and develop new versions of its software package. Porel is faced with a "chicken or the egg" type industry. The company must develop new products to keep pace with its competitors, yet in order to develop new programs the company must have cash to pay its specialized programmers. The only way to generate cash is through product sales.

In order to avoid large salary payments, Porel pays many of its key employees a bonus based on sales. Chen explains: "In spite of the obvious problems, the draw to the software industry has always been that once a program is developed, the incremental costs associated with the sale of each package are minimal."

The past year has seen a number of significant changes and events at Porel. The competition wars have taken their toll on Porel's cash reserves. The company has maxed out its bank loan balance and is in danger of breaching its loan covenants. As a result, for the first time Porel is considering issuing shares on the public market, using its soon-to-be-released November 30, 2000, year end financial statements.

MoneyMinders Inc. (MM) is a Canadian pension fund manager that specializes in the high-tech industry. MM is considering an investment in Porel and has approached you to review the company's accounting policies and the events that have occurred over the past year. MM expects you to recommend whether to invest in Porel.

You have spent the past two weeks at Porel and have learned the following:

1. Matthews has left the company after a disagreement with Chen over accounting policies. He has recently filed a $1 million lawsuit against Porel and Chen for wrongful dismissal. Chen contends that this suit is without merit and that Matthews will lose the case. No adjustment has been made to the financial statements.

2. Marila, Chen's wife, often purchases elaborate dresses using company monies. In the past these costs have been capitalized as assets and amortized over three years, since Chen believes they bring attention to the company — a sort of advertising. Marila is paid an annual salary of $100,000 for her services.

3. Sales for LetterPerfect software packages are recognized at the time of sale. In an attempt to gain market share, in September 1999 Porel added a 90-day money-back guarantee to all software packages. Chen does not intend to make any adjustments for potential returns, claiming the software is perfect.

4. In October 1999, Porel identified another potential revenue stream. The company began offering users the option to license its software and technical support for periods ranging from 1 to 10 years. Chen explains that this lease will allow users to receive upgrades and support as part of the lease payment. He is excited by this idea, pointing out: "There is virtually no additional cost for the service; I have the staff here anyway. All they have to do is lift the phone to answer questions while they are doing their other work." The company intends to record the leases as revenue at the time of contract signing.

5. Porel is developing a new product that Chen explains "will knock the socks off of MacroHard." He elaborates that over the past year he has spent at least 50% of his time on the new "Peanuts" platform and has therefore capitalized 50% of his $1 million salary to software development costs.

The managers at MM are very demanding and are not easily persuaded. Your report should include all the information that you feel is relevant to MM's investment decision and include a commentary on Porel's financial reporting methods.

## Required

Prepare the report that MM has requested.

# BUILT IT CORPORATION

## *A. Scilipoti*

Built It Corporation (BIC), a real estate developer, operates primarily in southern Ontario. The incorporated company has two shareholders, Larry Tremblay and Wendell MacDonald. The owners once played for the Toronto Maple Leafs. After successful hockey careers, they used their savings to start the company. Both are actively involved in managing the company.

BIC has been in existence for five years and has developed several residential and commercial buildings. BIC has two operating divisions: contract commercial and residential construction; and property management (i.e., collecting rents and maintaining properties).

BIC's operations have been financed primarily through an initial investment of $2 million by each of the shareholders and by a $10 million bank loan. The bank loan is secured against all of BIC's machinery and most of its properties under management. Certain bank covenants are attached to the loan. The company has been profitable since inception and has generated impressive positive cash flows from operations for all years except the first.

With economists predicting that the southern Ontario market will continue to boom, BIC is looking to expand its operations. It has won bids for several new contracts, and as a result the company is in desperate need of additional funds. BIC expects that it will require an additional $100 million. Neither shareholder wishes to use more of his own money. Both Larry and Wendell want to take BIC public in order to raise the funds. They realize that significant financial reporting and operational changes will be required.

Larry and Wendell have heard that you are presently taking an intensive university accounting course and are eager for your assistance. They have hired you to provide accounting policy recommendations and to point out any additional issues you feel will be relevant to their decision. BIC's financial year end is December 31.

Your preliminary investigation has revealed the following accounting issues:

1. Revenue on contract construction projects is usually recognized when title to the building has been transferred to the new buyers. Some buildings are finished within a year; other, larger buildings may take up to five years to construct. Most of the buildings developed by BIC are architecturally unique, as are the contract arrangements. However, Wendell is extremely conservative, and BIC does not recognize revenue until cash is received.

2. Residential rent is normally paid on a monthly basis; commercial tenants pay quarterly. Revenue on properties under management is recognized when cash is received. More recently, as the economy has softened, BIC has been having trouble collecting some of its rents. To date, the company has not taken any allowances for bad debt because they are not tax deductible.

3. Construction costs include any and all of the following:

- Material costs
- Labour costs
- Insurance costs
- Interest costs
- Cleaning costs
- Landscaping costs
- Zoning and licensing costs
- Management salaries
- Property taxes

Until this point in time, BIC has expensed all costs as they are incurred, except for material and labour costs, which are capitalized as part of the building asset account on the balance sheet.

4. During the past year the company capitalized a large assortment of costs associated with a new investment idea. Larry dreamed of constructing a new hockey arena for the Toronto Maple Leafs. BIC has expensed $2 million associated with the new project during the year.

5. All BIC sales managers are paid a bonus based on sales and are very anxious to see the new capital raised. Up to this point, BIC has had a difficult time retaining quality sales personnel.

6. Wendell's mother owns a separately incorporated property management company called Sugerdaddy Ltd. (SL). BIC sells most of its residential buildings to SL. Approximately 40% of most recent year end's revenues related to sales of buildings to SL.

## Required

1. Who are the users of BIC's financial statements? Indicate the individual needs and objectives of each, and indicate which of the noted objectives of accounting should be followed and why. Are there any constraints that should be followed? If so, explain why.

2. Review BIC's current accounting policies, and provide support for any recommended changes that may be necessary in light of your answer to Part 1.

# COMMUNICOM CORPORATION

## *A. Scilipoti*

Communicom Corporation ("Communicom") is a private Canadian company owned by Peter Jones. Peter used to work at Letron Corporation until he was let go as part of a corporate downsizing. In the early stages, Communicom was operated from Peter's basement in Kirkland Lake, Ontario. Two years ago, the company moved into a 25,000-square-foot facility. Communicom sells new and used phone equipment to local individuals and corporations, and installs it. It also sells, installs, and services data and voice communication equipment for local businesses. Peter says he has found a rural niche that the larger telecom companies have ignored.

The company's annual sales have doubled in the past year to $5 million. As a result of the company's rapid growth, Communicom has used up Peter's start-up capital of $1 million and the $1 million bank loan. The bank loan is secured by all of Peter's personal belongings. Peter is anxious to expand. He has been able to retain a very competent and dedicated sales and technical staff. However, he needs money to finance working capital for the longer-term system installations.

Peter needs to raise $2 million. In discussions with CIBC World Markets, a large Canadian brokerage house, he has been advised that he can raise the $2 million by issuing stock to the public in exchange for a 40% ownership interest in Communicom.

Peter has heard that you are taking an intensive accounting course and has asked you to recommend a course of action for Communicom to raise the necessary funds. Also, he needs you to recommend accounting policies and disclosure requirements for the upcoming year end financial statements based on your advice in this matter. You learn from a friend who lives in Kirkland Lake that Peter is a very demanding individual and that you will have to provide a sound, supported analysis if you hope to convince him to take your recommendations.

You accept the challenge and meet with Mary Potter, Communicom's chief financial officer, to discuss the company's financial reporting practices. You make the following notes:

1. The company has different collection terms for its customers depending on the type of services provided. Individuals must pay when services or products are delivered. Corporations are entitled to a 30-day credit term for equipment purchases, and a growing number of larger accounts have been given up to 18 months to pay for system installations. Most system installations take up to one year to complete. Mary explains that because Peter is very conservative, Communicom recognizes revenue only when cash is received. All receivables are reported as part of current assets.
2. Communicom buys new and used phone equipment. New equipment is purchased mainly from Letron; the used equipment is bought through auctions from bankrupt large corporations. Communicom technicians then refurbish the used equipment to ensure that it can be resold. The company includes only acquisition costs as part of inventory. Mary explains that the technicians would be needed anyway to manage the company's warranty.

3. Communicom offers both individuals and corporations a one-year warranty on purchased used equipment. In accordance with CRA guidelines, Communicom expenses its warranty costs on a cash basis as claims are processed.

4. Because Communicom has been expanding so rapidly, the company's staff use much of the telephone equipment internally. Mary explains that the equipment they use is reported as inventory on the company's balance sheet because it could always be sold later.

5. Peter's son, Tom, is vice-president of Communicom. Tom is a musician and is the company's highest-paid employee, with a salary of $100,000. In addition, Communicom pays for all of Tom's car and food expenses — and Peter's as well — because of the many hours both spend at the facility.

6. Sales managers are paid a bonus based on sales and are very anxious to see the additional capital raised.

7. While reviewing the legal expense file, you learn that Peter is in the middle of a divorce largely brought about by alleged affair with Mary. One of the legal invoices includes the following:

(a) $100,000 patent registration costs
(b) $50,000 divorce negotiations

All legal costs have been paid for and expensed by the company in the current year.

## Required

1. Outline the users of Communicom's financial statements. Indicate the individual needs and objectives of each. Which of the noted objectives of accounting should be followed, and why? Should any constraints be followed? If so, explain why.

2. Review Communicom's current accounting policies, and provide support for any changes that may be necessary in light of your answer in Part 1.

# DEADENT THEATRE COMPANY

## A. Scilipoti

After a successful acting career, the famous actor Darth Vader decided to open his own theatre company, Deadent Theatre Company ("Deadent"). Having had much experience in the theatrical business, he managed to raise $1,000,000 of equity investment from himself and five close friends. Vader remains Deadent's majority shareholder and president. At the beginning of the year, he also hired a general manager for $75,000 per year to oversee all productions and operations. Vader has indicated to you that he intends to list his company one day on the Toronto Stock Exchange in order to raise money for expansion into the United States.

During a recent visit to Toronto you run into Vader at a local nightclub. After hearing of your accounting expertise, he is eager for your assistance. He hires you to help finalize the company's September 30, 1999, year end financial statements and to provide recommendations for the issues noted below. Vader has advised you that no adjustments have been made for the listed transactions on the September 30, 1999, financial statements. He also wants your advice about the company's planned share issuance.

1. During the year, Deadent began building a new theatre in downtown Toronto. The following costs associated with the building's construction were fully paid as of September 30, 1999:

   (a) Materials                  $250,000
   (b) Labour                      450,000
   (c) Architectural drawings      75,000
   (d) Vader estimates that the general manager spent four months of the past year directly on the construction of the new theatre.
   (e) The land for the building's construction was donated by Paramount, Vader's former employer. Vader thinks the value of the land is $300,000. The building was completed May 1, 1999.

2. During the year, Deadent began rehearsing and preparing for its first live show, *Shag Time*. Deadent paid the following costs associated with this production:

   (a) $200,000 for set construction. Vader points out that the set is versatile enough that he will be able to use it for many other productions.
   (b) Rehearsal costs, including makeup, etc., of $400,000.

3. *Shag Time* is a world-renowned production and has generated $600,000 in ticket sales since its debut on May 1, 1999. Deadent has entered into contracts with the show's actors to pay them a salary equal to 50% of total revenues. During the rehearsal time, prior to May 1, 1999, Deadent paid the same actors a total of $150,000 in wages.

4. Deadent received a $100,000 legal bill — fully paid as of September 30, 1999 — for services rendered during the period ended September 30, 1999. The bill was subdivided as follows:

(a) $20,000 for incorporation costs.

(b) $25,000 to register the patents associated with the new show.

(c) $55,000 for work related to the divorce settlement between Vader and his estranged wife Monica.

You have decided to accept the engagement and have learned that Vader is a very demanding individual who is not easily persuaded. He will require a detailed analysis of your recommended accounting policies in light of the pending financing decision.

## Required

Provide your report to Mr. Vader.

# ENDLESS BEAUTY LIMITED

## A. Scilipoti

Steven Lindman is an extremely successful antique dealer in Fredericton, New Brunswick. After immigrating from Scotland, he began his operation, Endless Beauty Limited (EBL), by selling his own family heirlooms. On retiring five years ago, he gave his son John authority to carry on the family business.

John took EBL across the country, opening outlets in each major city. EBL went public at the beginning of last year, selling 25% of the business on the Canadian market. Since then sales have doubled along with the number of retail locations and the company's share price. But John is still not satisfied. He wants to sell an additional 20% of the company to a private equity fund, Braindrain Fund.

Braindrain has asked for your advice on its investment decision. It expects a detailed analysis in which you provide concrete support for your recommendation.

After a long discussion with John and Steven you learn the following:

1. Steven purchased the building in which EBL operates in 1950 when he arrived in Canada. The building is in downtown Fredericton and is entirely paid for.
2. EBL maintains a working line of credit with a local chartered bank that is fully secured by the building described in 1.
3. EBL also operates two historic sites outside Fredericton. One of the buildings has been converted into a hotel; the other is leased from the local government.
4. The hotel was purchased in 1961 for $200,000 and was valued at $2.5 million at the initial public offering (IPO). Prior to the IPO the hotel was not profitable. Since then, EBL has been selling multivisit contracts to hotel guests at a discount. John explains that the contracts can be used over a period of three years. EBL records revenue on the contracts at the time of sale.
5. The second building, an army base, is held on a 15-year lease, which expires in 2015. The value of the building was approximately $28 million at the time of the IPO. Since then, the army base has proved to be a significant part of EBL's income. The building is reported as an operating lease. EBL is responsible for all maintenance costs and has the option to purchase the army base for $30 million in 2059. Previously, revenue was booked monthly as it came due. However, John has changed the policy over the past year, asserting the government will pay. Revenue is now booked in three-year increments to correspond to the lease term.
6. EBL purchases the bulk of its merchandise from estate and garage sales, as well as at auctions and bankruptcy sales. Items are usually purchased as part of a group. Since the IPO, margins have increased and inventory turns have slowed. John has told you not to worry about the slower inventory turns and to focus on the margin growth.
7. Antiques are often sent out to John's uncle, Philip, to be refinished or restored before they are sold. Phillip and Steven have been known to exchange services rather than cash.

8. Because of Steven's notoriety in the community, customers have been offered extended payment terms. It is not uncommon for Steven to allow customers two or three years to pay for purchases. Revenues are always booked on delivery.

## Required

Prepare a report to Braindrain, with detailed reasons for your recommendations.

# IGLOO CORPORATION

## *A. Scilipoti*

Igloo Corporation ("Igloo") was incorporated in Canada in 1950. Igloo is in the software development business. Until it went public in June 1995, the company was owned by Mr. Magoo. Since then the company's revenues have increased over 25% per year even while its income has *decreased* by 10% per year. As a result, since reaching a high of $100 the company's share price has fallen to $25.

The company currently maintains a bank loan that requires a maximum debt-to-equity ratio of 2:1. As of the company's December 31, 2004, year end, the company's debt balance is $3.6 million and its equity balance is $2 million. Igloo requires additional financing to continue its research and development and for various operating needs. Mr. Magoo's daughter, Sally, a recent University of Toronto graduate, has designed a new form of debt financing called no-yield-option notes (NYONs). Igloo intends to issue the $2 million in NYONs on February 15, 2004. The details of the NYONs are as follows:

1. The NYONs mature on February 15, 202X.
2. Each NYON will be purchased for $200 and have a maturity value of $200.
3. Each can be converted into common shares of the company after being held for one year at a ratio of eight common shares for each NYON. The conversion is at the company's option.
4. The NYONs will yield a 10% annual interest payment.

At a recent board meeting, Magoo is excited. He explains that the NYONs will be recorded as equity. He announces that Igloo's income for year end 2005 is expected to be 15% of revenue and that the company's share price will soon "rise beyond your wildest imagination!"

## Required

Retired Inc., a pension fund, is interested in long-term investments and currently owns 15% of Igloo's common shares. You have been retained by Retired to comment on the proposed NYONs. It has asked you to provide detailed support for your comments as well as recommendations to pass on at the upcoming shareholders' meeting.

# JACK B. NIMBLE

## *A. Scilipoti*

Your friend, Jack B. Nimble, started a small restaurant business in his basement over the summer. Since Jack lives near the university, he expects that many students will be drawn to his inexpensive home-cooked meals. Having heard that you are taking an intensive accounting course, he of course has asked for your help in preparing some accounting information for his first year, ended August 31, 2002.

To start the business, he installed a "professional" oven/range in his home for $5,000. Also, he acquired a mixer, various pans, and other cooking and baking utensils for $1,200. To finance the acquisition of these items, he borrowed $10,000 at 10% interest from the local bank. The loan was taken out on April 1, 2002, and is repayable on December 31, 2002.

It is now September 1, 2002. Jack says he is very pleased with the growth of the business and thinks his "bank account looks pretty good."

A review of the business's bank account statements shows the following:

- Deposits in the bank from customers totalled $9,500.
- The following cheques were written: ingredients and food supplies, $3,500; miscellaneous small items such as aprons, oven mitts and spices, $150; repairs to the oven, $150; utilities (gas and hydro), $180.
- The wear and tear on the oven is estimated at $500.
- A review of credit card slips indicates that the business still owes $230 for food.
- A review of Jack's invoices shows that a customer still owes the business $350 for services rendered in late August.

Jack is considering expanding to the rest of his home at some point in the future.

## Required

1. Prepare an income statement (in good form) for Jack's business for the period ended August 31, 2002. Make all relevant assumptions. In addition, list the questions and issues you need to resolve with Jack before you can finalize the financial statements. In other words, what additional information do you require in order to provide helpful financial statements?
2. Discuss Jack's assessment of his performance.
3. What other financial information do you think would be relevant to Jack? Explain.

# JOKEMON INC.

## A. Scilipoti

While sitting at home one evening after an exhilarating day at business school, you receive a telephone call from an old friend of yours, Monica Persky. Monica, a history major, is in a financial predicament and requires your expert accounting advice with respect to a business she has started recently. You agree to meet her for lunch the next day and learn the following about her company:

Jokemon Inc. ("Jokemon") was incorporated on October 1, 2000, under Canadian federal corporate legislation. Monica is the sole shareholder, owning 100% of the common shares of the company.

Jokemon develops, manufactures, and distributes a unique stuffed animal and other toys named Jokemon. The company has grown very rapidly since inception, capitalizing on the recent boom in the home entertainment market. Monica informs you that the success of this industry is linked directly to the state of the economy and, more specifically, to the levels of personal disposable income.

The industry is also fiercely competitive, with thousands of toy developers and producers worldwide targeting the same market as Jokemon. Monica says "it seems that new toys are popping up on the market each day." From this, you determine that the development of new, high-quality toys is crucial for the long-term survival of Jokemon. To entice and retain her employees, Monica has offered certain key staff bonuses based on the net income of the company.

Monica informs you that the company is almost out of cash. Unless it can access cash immediately, it will not be able to fund further product development. She also informs you that her personal bank account is empty and that she has approached her bank for financing.

Monica desperately needs your advice. Financial statements must be prepared for the bank. Attached (page 135) is the *adjusted* trial balance of Jokemon for the year that ended September 30, 2001.

## Required

Bill, the previous controller of Jokemon, was fired after a scandal involving Monica. You have agreed to help Monica prepare the September 30, 2001, year end financial statements.

1. List the users of Jokemon's financial statements. Indicate the individual needs and objectives of each. Which of the noted objectives of accounting should be followed, and why? Should any constraints be followed? If so, explain why.
2. Prepare the balance sheet and income statement pursuant to the bank's request. Where necessary or appropriate (i.e., only where there is choice in the accounting treatment), provide Monica with the reasons for your accounting treatment, using the facts-constraints-objectives framework. Remember to tie back to your answers in Part 1.
3. Assume the role of banker. Would you provide Jokemon with additional financing? Explain why.

## Jokemon Inc. Adjusted Trial Balance as at September 30, 2001

| | Debt | Credit |
|---|---:|---:|
| Cash | $ 1,000 | |
| Accounts receivable | 80,000 | |
| Research and development costs | 70,000 | |
| Inventory | 185,000 | |
| Unexpired insurance | 1,400 | |
| Property, computer hardware/software* | 200,000 | |
| Selling, general, and administration | 182,900 | |
| Bad debts expense | 12,000 | |
| Amortization expense | 30,000 | |
| Interest expense | 16,000 | |
| Income tax expense | 3,525 | |
| Cost of goods sold | 255,000 | |
| Sales | | $ 515,000 |
| Common shares | | 30,000 |
| Accumulated amortization | | 50,000 |
| Allowance for doubtful accounts | | 12,000 |
| Loan due to shareholder | | 200,000 |
| Accounts payable & accrued liabilities | | 160,300 |
| Retained earnings | | 50,000 |
| Interest payable | | 16,000 |
| Income taxes payable | | 3,525 |
| **Total** | **$ 1,036,825** | **$ 1,036,825** |

*At historical cost. Fair market value is estimated at $150,000.

# LET YOUR BACKBONE SLIDE

## *A. Scilipoti*

Fresh after being stripped of the gold medal at the 2000 Winter Olympics in downhill skiing, Mike Rigatoni decided to use his corporate sponsorship income and his skiing knowledge to make money. He teamed up with Guy Whosien, a prominent Vancouver real estate developer, to enter the ski resort business.

In 2000, Mike and Guy incorporated Let Your Backbone Slide Inc. (LYBSI) as equal shareholders. Both men initially invested $500,000 each in the new venture. Their goal was to grow rapidly by acquiring existing ski resorts and, ultimately, take LYBSI public within two years.

Mike was able to use his skiing contacts, and Guy his real estate experience, with great success. Based on preliminary financial statements for the company's December 31, 2001, year end, LYBSI's revenues had grown to $1.5 million. By the end of 2001, LYBSI had acquired five resorts using $2 million in debt financing. The company's sales are seasonal, and Guy predicts that LYBSI will need to sell shares to the public by the spring of 2002.

In light of the company's need for equity financing, Mike and Guy have not finalized the December 31, 2001, year end financial statements. During a recent visit to Toronto, you run into Mike and Guy at a local nightclub. After hearing that you are taking accounting, they are eager for your assistance. They have hired you to review and advise the company on its current accounting policies for the 2001 year end. Furthermore, since the old statements will be used as part of the public offering, they ask you to document any additional information regarding the company's planned share issuance that you think might be important to them.

Over the past two weeks you have learned the following:

1. Recently, in January 2002, *Forbes Magazine* described LYBSI as the "largest ski resort operator in North America." The media attention enabled Mike to hire his former ski team members, and Guy his old property managers, in exchange for a percentage of sales. Furthermore, other ski resorts have been approaching LYBSI to be bought out. Mike and Guy think the news of the added employees and prospective purchases should be shown as assets of the company.

2. Also in January 2002, an avalanche occurred at the company's Yeller resort in British Columbia. Mike assures you that Yeller, the company's largest resort, will be operational by the end of February. The repair costs are estimated at $500,000 to $750,000. No adjustments have been made to the 1999 year end statements.

3. LYSBI sells passes to members that can be used throughout the ski season. Discounts are offered to members who book beyond one season. Payments are made evenly over the life of the pass. Revenue is recognized when contracts are signed. Recently, the company added a 60-day money-back guarantee for its season pass holders. Guy explained: "We are so confident in the fun you will have at LYBSI that no one will ask for their money back!" No adjustments have been made to the 2001 financial statements.

4. LYBSI purchases land for two main purposes: to develop ski resorts, and to build and sell condos on the properties to encourage more frequent attendance. Guy is especially proud of LYBSI's most recent development in Alaska: "I've spent 50% of my time over the past year and invested over 60% of the company's money in the new condo project on the Alaskan site. People will come to the resort!" Currently, 50% of Guy's $100,000 salary and 60% of the company's interest costs have been capitalized to buildings held for sale. The balances of the two amounts have been capitalized to land costs.

5. According to Mike, "LYBSI has always been able to show a 'healthy' three-to-one current ratio and year over year, income has increased by over 50%. Investors should be excited to be part of our growing balance sheet." Ski lifts and buildings are depreciated over 50 years.

6. Guy has recently purchased, from LYSBI, a plot of land near one of the company's resorts. The sale resulted in a $1 million gain for LYSBI in 2001. The total sale price of $1.5 million was settled with a three-year non-interest-bearing note receivable from Guy.

Mike and Guy are very demanding individuals and are not easily persuaded. They require a detailed analysis of the pros and cons of each of the accounting policies you recommend in light of the financing decision.

## Required

Prepare the report that Mike and Guy requested.

# LITTLE JOHNNY'S BOOK BARN

## A. Scilipoti

Little Johnny's Book Barn (LJBB), owned by the Reading family, was incorporated under federal corporate legislation several years ago. In the past year, 1998, the Readings have decided to take a more passive role in the company's wholesale book business and to let its three managers run each location. To ensure their good judgment, the Readings have decided to offer them a 10% bonus based on the company's net income before taxes.

The managers are confused and have asked for your advice on whether to accept the Readings' offer. You have since compiled the following information about the company's financial accounting policies:

1. LJBB has always sold two types of books: special editions and regular stock. For special editions, revenue is recognized when the sale occurs. These books are sold on a "no-return, final-sale" basis. Revenue on regular stock is recognized when the return period of 10 months elapses because customers are allowed to return 50%, at retail price, of the regular stock they purchased over the previous 10 months.
2. LJBB has always depreciated its buildings and equipment using income tax methods and rates. Maximum rates and amounts have always been claimed, which has resulted in a larger accumulated amortization figure than if straight-line amortization had been used.
3. Mr. Reading has been involved in some potential employee disputes. LJBB has recorded a provision of $400,000 for potential legal costs in its current fiscal period.

## Required

Provide a report to the managers to assist them with their decision. Provide support for your recommendations.

# MICHAEL SERVICES INC.

## A. Scilipoti

Michael, a friend of yours from undergraduate days, has recently purchased a small metal-recycling company from Two Brothers Incorporated (TB). He has incorporated the company under the name Michael Services Inc. (MSI). Michael is a dreamer, and in order to achieve his goals, he will need money. However, he is unsure what type of financing will be best, given his current circumstances.

After a long review and discussion with the previous owners, Michael has approached you to advise him on appropriate accounting policies for MSI. The following is a summary of Michael's notes:

1. TB entered into long leases for the use of its processing equipment. The leases are coming due in the next few months.
2. Purchases of scrap metal are by the truckload. Each truckload may have different types of metal, each with varying values.
3. Scrap metal can be sold to other scrap dealers or it can be processed and sold to end users. Final sale prices are based on the final weight and are determined when the product arrives at the client's site.
4. Metal prices go up and down. The previous year, TB was stockpiling copper because of its low price. Unfortunately, the current year has seen prices fall another 25%, and TB has not taken any provisions.
5. TB often exchanged scrap metal for reprocessed/recycled metal.

## Required

Prepare the report to Michael, giving full reasoning for your recommendations.

# VINTAGE WINERY

## A. Scilipoti

Shortly after her great-grandfather died, Sofia inherited the family corporation, Vintage Winery (VW). Mr. Uva started VW over fifty years ago, just after immigrating from Italy.

Mr. Uva was a shrewd man. For example, he never recorded revenue until cash was received, and he refused to take on any debt or outside investment for expansion purposes. His motto was "I will not buy what I cannot afford."

Sofia has worked in the business from a very young age, and now that Mr. Uva has passed away she is eager to take the business to new levels. Already, the largest Canadian wine distributor, Bottles Corp., is interested in marketing Vintage's special blends throughout the United States.

Sofia is anxious because she realizes she will be unable to produce enough wine on her great-grandfather's estate. She will need money to purchase neighbouring properties and as working capital. She is more adventurous than her grandfather but has much of his savvy. She has asked you to help her establish new accounting policies for preparing financial statements, which will be used for an offering. Specifically, she is concerned about the following:

1. She is prepared to raise $5 million through a new public financing vehicle called GRAPEs (great rate annuity payment equity). The GRAPEs will pay an 8% annual dividend and will be repayable after five years. Prior to expiry, at the option of the holder, each $1,000 GRAPE will be convertible into VW common shares at $40 per share. At expiry, the company has the right to repay the GRAPEs at the same exchange rate or cash. Vintage does not currently trade publicly, so there is no current market price for the shares. Sofia is not sure how the GRAPEs should be accounted for.

2. All maintenance and land care costs have been expensed as incurred. The vineyards have not been depreciated.

3. All bottled wine has been recorded as a capital asset because Mr. Uva always held back seasonal production on a biannual basis. That is, he sold 2000 wine in 2002, 2001 in 2003, and so on. Sometimes certain vintages were held for five years or more.

## Required

Prepare the report for Sofia.

# ZERENSKY'S AWESOME PANTS

## *Kevin Markle*

Zerensky's Awesome Pants Ltd. (ZAP) was incorporated by Karen Zerensky 10 years ago. The company makes a wide variety of pants, skirts, and shorts for men, women, and children. Karen owns all of the company's common shares. The company struggled at or below the break-even point for the first few years, but then earned a large profit four years ago when Karen correctly predicted that the trend among young men to wear pants that look like they are falling off would continue and focused heavily on that niche. Since then, the company has consistently turned a profit of over $100,000 per year and has started to pay Karen salary and dividends totalling more than $75,000 each year.

Ms. Barrow, a wealthy investor with an interest in the fashion industry, has recently approached Karen about making an equity investment in ZAP. Barrow believes that ZAP is poised to go to the next level of success and that her equity investment and experience are the two elements that it needs to take it there. Barrow has offered Karen $300,000 for 40% of the common shares of the company. Barrow has said that she does not require regular dividends and would prefer that the money be left in the company to generate growth. Barrow does not want to incur the cost and hassle of valuing the company, so she has offered a price that she knows is in excess of the market value. Karen agrees that the price is more than fair.

Ms. Barrow does, however, have concerns about the company's financial statements. Karen explains that she has always prepared the financial statements for the sole purpose of filing them with the tax return. Barrow explains that she, as a minority equity investor, requires financial statements that she can use to evaluate the performance of the company in order to decide when she needs to provide her input on operational issues. Based on what she knows already, her first suggestion is that ZAP take advantage of the low interest rates in the market and obtain a large ($500,000 or more) loan to be used for financing further growth.

Karen has come to you for your advice on ZAP's financial statements. She has already decided to accept Ms. Barrow's offer for the shares, and she agrees that obtaining a loan would be a good idea. She is is not sure what changes need to be made to the policies for preparing financial statements and would like you to provide her with a report containing your recommendations on specific issues. She is a businesswoman, not an accountant, but she makes it clear to you that she wants to fully understand the reasoning behind your recommendations.

You review the financial statements and records of the company and find the following:

1. ZAP buys fabric from several different suppliers. Because it is almost impossible to predict what will be popular in any given season of any given year, the profit margins can be greatly improved if ZAP can buy large quantities of a fabric before its market price increases due to increased demand. That is why Karen has always tried to read trends and buy in advance. At each year end she looks at the inventory on hand and writes off

anything that will likely not be used. However, ZAP rarely throws fabric out as it can usually be held until a new style that uses it comes around.

2. ZAP owns its warehouse and many of its machines. Karen has always just used the tax amortization rates set by the government tax office for accounting because it is simple.

3. ZAP has an agreement with its major customers that it will fully refund the cost of any goods that are returned because they are damaged or flawed. Because she was advised that any accruals of these costs would not be allowed for tax purposes, Karen has never recorded any and instead has recorded the refunds as selling costs in the years in which they were paid.

4. A major retail clothing chain filed a lawsuit against ZAP six months ago claiming that ZAP had infringed on its copyrighted name. It is suing for $1 million plus a requirement for ZAP to change its name. ZAP's lawyer is not sure how the case will turn out but has suggested to Karen that the competitor might want to settle out of court. He has approached the plaintiff, and it has indicated that it will not settle for less than $300,000. Karen has decided that it is worth going to trial. Her lawyer has said the trial will not likely happen for at least two years due to backlog in the courts. Nothing related to the lawsuit is reported in the financial statements.

5. In the early years of the company's operations, Karen's father wanted to help out and made $100,000 available to her. Wanting things to be done properly, Karen decided to have ZAP issue nonvoting preferred shares to her father in exchange for the cash. The preferred shares pay a cumulative dividend of 6% and are redeemable at the option of her father. Under the agreement, ZAP must redeem the shares by March 31, 2010. They are currently shown in the shareholders' equity section of the balance sheet.

## Required

Prepare the report for Karen Gillam.

# BOMBADEER CO.

## *Arthur R. Guimaraes*

Bombadeer Co. (BC) is a family owned, private company with two manufacturing divisions: Train and Airplane. BC recently got out of the auto industry. Each of the divisions has its own management team; however, all major decisions (including reporting and financing) are overseen by the family. The company was established more than 85 years ago and has operations in various countries.

The family has recently decided to pursue an initial public offering (IPO) of the Train Division, which will involve the division "going public," with Ester & Associates as the investment advisors. Management will receive significant stock options from the deal. The family has no plans to take the Airplane Division public, given the weak state of the industry. You have received correspondence from a recent investment advisory meeting, where Ester & Associates was quoted as saying: "Given BC has always selected conservative accounting policies to conserve cash, now is your time to dress up the statements . . . We want to get a good price for the Train Division based on an earnings valuation and show your creditors how much this division is really worth."

You have been contacted by the family to review, and if applicable update, BC's accounting policies. You have significant experience in the manufacturing sector. You have been provided with the following information:

## Planes

The Airplane Division has seen revenue decline in recent years as a result of the slowdown in the airline industry. BC's customers are mostly commercial airlines, which have been operating in a very difficult environment and as a result have actually been cancelling orders for airplanes. Other companies have defaulted on payments. As a result, BC has seen its inventory of planes rise, and sales are becoming less predictable.

## Trains

The Train Division has historically been the more consistent of the divisions. Its motto is "the tortoise won the race." The industry has recently gone through a boom period, given increased consolidation and growing demand for trains throughout the world. Order cancellations are rare. By far the biggest client of the Train Division is governments.

## All Divisions

Both divisions have historically recognized revenue at the latest point possible. The process for selling includes getting an order, which may occur one year before payment is received. A 25% deposit is received six months from delivery. The plane or train is then delivered. Normally two months after delivery, BC is paid in full.

BC depreciates its buildings using rates recommended by the CRA.

## Required

Provide recommendations for any changes in accounting policies that you think are appropriate.

# BOOKS4U INC.

## K. Bewley

Books4U Inc. (B4U) was incorporated many years ago and its common shares are publicly traded. B4U operates a number of large retail bookstores across the country. In 2000, B4U started up a subsidiary Internet business, called Books.com, to handle online book sales. Books.com also provides advertising and promotions for other online retailer's websites; in return, they provide advertising for Books.com on their own sites. Several executive managers of B4U have received options to purchase common shares of B4U at a fixed price of $10 per share. The options expire in 2009. B4U shares are currently trading at $14.

It is now late 2001 and the consolidated financial results are being prepared for B4U's year ended November 30, 2001. You are a financial analyst who follows B4U and reports to investors on its future prospects. You recently met with B4U's managers and reviewed their preliminary financial statements for the year ended November 30, 2001. Those statements included the following items:

1. Books.com recognized advertising revenues of $1 million for advertising several other online retailing companies on the Books.com website. In exchange, Books.com obtained $1 million worth of advertising on these same other companies' websites. B4U's managers believe that this bartering was an astute business move that "saves us tons of cash and generates revenues at the same time." Management has added a line to the B4U accounting policy note to the effect that "advertising revenues are recognized when earned."

2. Books.com used promotions to bring people to its website. For example, customers who bought a pizza from a national pizza chain received a coupon for $10 off their next Books.com purchase. Management accounted for these costs as marketing expenses instead of recording them as a cost of goods sold because, in their view, "the gross profit line is very sensitive in the retailing industry, so it is preferable to show these expenses below the gross profit line." Other Books.com expenditures included in "marketing expenses" are costs of warehousing and packaging goods and shipping them to customers.

3. Books.com's revenues and assets are a material component of B4U's financial position and results. B4U's managers believe that all their operations are in the same line of business — book retailing — and that therefore there is no need to provide segmented information in their audited financial statement notes.

## Required

As an analyst of B4U's financial performance, comment on management's accounting choices for the above issues. State your position, giving reasons that support it. In particular, consider the information's impact on investors in B4U publicly traded common shares.

# CHERIE CORPORATION

## *Prem M. Lobo*

Cherie Corporation (CC) is a Canadian private company based in Edmonton. CC owns and operates a chain of bookstores in cities across Canada and maintains a website where customers can order books online. CC also develops and publishes specialty books for niche markets. Cherie has experienced rapid growth in the past few years and is known in the industry for its aggressive marketing and its attention to customer service.

Joe Megabucks, a wealthy investor, is interested in acquiring a controlling interest in CC. He has hired you to help him analyze the financial statements as part of his overall due diligence procedures prior to finalizing his proposed purchase. In particular, Joe has presented you with the following information:

### Cherie Corporation
### In millions

| For the fiscal years: | 2002 | 2001 |
|---|---|---|
| Sales | 1000 | 800 |
| Cost of sales | 500 | 400 |
| Gross margin | 500 | 400 |
| | | |
| Selling and admin expenses | 150 | 100 |
| Interest expense | 100 | 90 |
| Depreciation and amortization | 50 | 40 |
| Total expenses | 300 | 230 |
| Net income before taxes | 200 | 170 |

1. Customers using CC's website can purchase books online and pay for them by credit card. Orders are shipped within 24 hours. CC records revenue on sales when books are shipped to the customer.
2. Cherie receives government assistance in the form of cash for certain books it publishes that promote "Canadian heritage and culture." Government assistance is recorded as revenue when persuasive evidence of an arrangement with the government exists, cash receipts can be estimated, collection is assured, and development of the book in question is complete and publication is about to commence.
3. Cash interest paid was $150 million in 2001 and $180 million in 2002.
4. CC capitalizes all costs associated with the research and development of its line of specialty books. As of 2002, capitalized development costs amounted to $150 million.
5. The breakdown of 2002 revenues is as follows:

| | |
|---|---|
| Book store sales | $500,000,000 |
| Internet sales | 400,000,000 |
| Government assistance | 50,000,000 |

6. In 2000, CC decided to engage in a strategic relationship with Webber Books, an online distributor. CC acquired a 35% stake in Webber for cash of $250,000,000. As part of the strategic agreement, CC and Webber agreed to integrate their information systems and Webber committed to purchasing $150,000,000 worth of books from CC commencing in 2002 for sale through its own distribution network.
7. Included in selling and administrative expenses are head-office overhead costs, delivery and order fulfillment costs for Internet customers, and head office salaries.
8. Amortization of development costs occurs once a specialty book is ready for publication and sale. Capitalized development costs are amortized each year based on the ratio of current revenue from specialty books to expected total future revenue from specialty books over a period not exceeding eight years.
9. Industry gross margins average around 30% of sales.

## Required

Identify any concerns that Joe Megabucks should have with respect to the financial information of CC presented above. Provide full reasons why they should concern Joe. Also, identify any additional information that Joe will require, with explanations as to why this information should be relevant to him.

# CREATIVE CRIBS INC.

## *V. Umashanker Trivedi*

Dorothy and Chris Ah-fat formed Creative Cribs Inc. (CCI) this year and are its sole shareholders. The idea for CCI originated when Chris, who is good with his hands, constructed a retro-looking crib when their new son James was born three years ago. All their acquaintances marvelled at the crib and wanted one built for their own children. For the past three years Chris has been obliging them by building these retro cribs in his garage. However, given the increasing interest in the crib and a demographic change suggesting a baby boom in the next few years, both Dorothy and Chris have quit their respective jobs this year and started CCI using their pooled savings of $250,000. The bank has extended a line of credit to CCI based on personal guarantees provided by Dorothy and Chris, who are using their home (co-owned by both) as collateral. Other details about CCI:

1. CCI produces two types of cribs: Elegant and Luxury. The Luxury is nothing but the Elegant version with some add-ons and modifications. For retail sales, Elegant is priced at $1,500, while Luxury is priced at $2,800. CCI has entered into an agreement with a manufacturer in China to manufacture and ship Elegant to its head office. Chris uses a few hired hands to convert Elegant models into Luxury models after they arrive in this country. Additional materials for this conversion are purchased locally. While it is possible to reconvert the Luxury models back to Elegant models, this process is time consuming and labour intensive and requires CCI to pay workers at 1½ times regular pay rates.

2. CCI had to pay an upfront nonrefundable fee of $50,000 to the manufacturer in China so that it could reconfigure its factory space in order to manufacture the Elegant line of cribs. The agreement between CCI and the manufacturer makes the latter the exclusive supplier of the cribs to CCI for five years. CCI has the option, at the end of the five years, to extend this contract for an additional three years by paying an additional upfront fee of $25,000 at that time.

3. CCI has entered into a lease agreement to rent office and factory space in a neighbouring industrial/office complex for three years. The monthly rent is $400 plus 0.5% of net sales. CCI had to pay an interest-free refundable deposit of $15,000 to the landlord when signing the lease. Also, 25% of the factory space has been converted into a warehouse to store the Elegant and Luxury models. The remaining 75% is used to manufacture the Luxury model.

4. Dorothy is in charge of receivables, payroll, marketing, and finance; Chris is in charge of payables, manufacturing, quality control, and interacting with the supplier in China.

5. Both Dorothy and Chris have drawn only the barest minimum cash from CCI to meet their living expenses, the point being to conserve the cash recourses of CCI.

6. CCI has entered into an agreement with a local chain of discount stores. That chain will carry the Elegant and Luxury cribs, with the right to return unsold cribs to CCI.

Chris feels that returned models of Elegant can be resold without any problem; however, there may not be a large enough market for all returned Luxury models. So if returns are high, some of these returned Luxury models may have to be reconverted back to the Elegant models and resold at their usual price.

7. Neither Dorothy nor Chris has an accounting background. CCI has just completed its first anniversary in business. Dorothy and Chris realize that they have to come up with a set of financial statements. So they have approached you, the "accounting guru," for advice about appropriate accounting policies, procedures, and records that CCI needs to maintain.

## Required

Write a report to CCI. In it, include your advice to them on the appropriate accounting policies, procedures, and records they need to follow and maintain.

# WALLACE INC.

## *Prem M. Lobo*

Wallace Inc. ("Wallace") is a medium-sized manufacturer of auto parts. Wallace was founded about 15 years ago by Peter Wallace, who began manufacturing auto components under the brand names of national retailers such as American Tire and WalSmart.

The company is wholly owned by Wallace and his wife, Samantha. Peter has recently experienced a midlife crisis and wants to leave the automotive business for something more exciting. After long discussions, Peter and Samantha have decided to sell their shares in Wallace.

They have been approached by a prospective buyer, who wants to see a set of audited GAAP financial statements before agreeing to buy. Until now, Wallace's financial statements have been prepared strictly to calculate income taxes.

It is now March 2003, and the financial results for the year ended December 31, 2002, are being finalized. You have been retained by Peter and Samantha to provide advice on the selection of appropriate accounting policies for the financial statements that will be prepared for the prospective buyer. They want full explanations for any recommendations you make. You learn the following:

1. Wallace has three significant customers who together account for 80% of total revenues. Total revenues for the 2002 fiscal year were $15 million.
2. Wallace maintains a significant inventory in order to respond to customer orders on a timely basis. Inventory is recorded at cost. During discussions with Peter, you discover that about $50,000 of inventory has been sitting in a factory for over a year; it comprises parts for products that are currently not being manufactured.
3. The company expensed $2 million on R&D during 2002. Most of this amount was spent on a project to develop a new shock mechanism for automobiles. Peter authorized this expenditure after discussions with American Tire during which American Tire expressed an interest in carrying a line of shocks. Wallace has never manufactured shocks before, and the project has experienced difficulties, particularly in getting the specifications right. Peter is optimistic that these initial difficulties will be overcome and has allocated a further $2 million to see the project to completion.
4. In fiscal 2001, Wallace's main competitor, Autoparts Inc., launched legal proceedings against Wallace, claiming that Wallace had infringed on its patents for certain automobile components. Autoparts is demanding $5 million for lost profits and punitive damages. Wallace's lawyers indicate that the actual amount should be $1 million and that the lawsuit could be settled out of court for $500,000. Wallace's lawyers indicate that there is a 50% chance of winning the lawsuit if it goes to trial. No amount has been recorded in the financial statements for this lawsuit.
5. On December 31, 2002, Wallace sold its old production equipment and leased new equipment from Leasing Inc. The lease signed was for an initial term of seven years, with a renewal term of three years, and included a monthly lease payment of $100,000. The present value of these lease payments at the inception of the lease was $7 million.

The new equipment has a useful life of 14 years and a fair market value of $8 million. The equipment is integral to Wallace's operations, and similar equipment is difficult to locate. Wallace agreed to perform all repairs and maintenance on the equipment during the life of the lease. The lease has cancellation provisions.

6. At January 1, 2002, on its balance sheet, Wallace reported capital assets (other than production equipment) as follows:

- Cost — $10 million
- Accumulated amortization — $5 million.

During 2002, Wallace reported amortization of these capital assets of $1 million. The tax value of these capital assets at January 1, 2002, was $5 million. During 2002, Wallace claimed a tax credit for amortization on these capital assets of $2 million.

Wallace does not currently employ future income tax methods of accounting, and has not reported future income tax liabilities or assets at December 31, 2002.

The tax rate in 2002 was 30%, and the expected tax rate for the foreseeable future is 25%.

## Required

Prepare a report to Peter and Samantha Wallace based on your analyses.

# LIBERTY HEALTH NETWORK INC.

*Alan T. Mak*

Liberty Health Network Inc. ("Liberty") is a for-profit tertiary care facility (i.e., a community hospital) operator based in Calgary. Liberty was founded in 2004 by a group of successful doctors, who believe that privatized health care is inevitable. The doctors see Liberty becoming a nationwide hospital operator modelled after successful American health care companies. Liberty expects to raise capital from the public markets in order to finance its rapid expansion.

Liberty's first (and currently, only) facility is in the Calgary Foothills community. An excerpt from Liberty's business plan for Foothills is provided in the appendix.

In preparing for its first year end, Liberty has retained you as an accounting consultant. Expectations are high for Liberty, and many eyes around the country are watching to tout, or tease, the company as the first large-scale private hospital.

You have been asked to advise on how the company should treat the following:

1. Liberty is projecting a loss for income tax purposes of approximately $700,000 for its first year of operations. This figure includes a $250,000 charge for capital cost allowance (CCA), which is the "temporary" difference between its tax and accounting cost bases. CCA is a discretionary deduction (meaning that the company does not have to claim the deduction, in part or in whole). Liberty will probably elect to not deduct CCA in its first year of operations. What amount, if any, should Liberty report as a future tax asset?

2. Like many other Canadian hospitals, Liberty must compete fiercely to attract talented doctors. As an incentive to join Liberty's staff, Liberty pays its new recruits a one-time signing bonus of $50,000. In exchange, the doctor must provide 1,000 hours of care at Liberty. There are no time limits attached to the care delivery period. Some doctors fulfill their requirements in eight months; others don't satisfy their contracts for several years. How should the incentive payments be reported on Liberty's financial statements?

3. As part of its election platform, the federal government is providing substantial subsidies and grants to hospitals that make investments in specific areas of infrastructure. Liberty's purchase of a magnetic resonance imaging (MRI) machine qualified for a $300,000 grant. How should the grant be reported?

## Required

Prepare your report to Liberty's CFO.

# Appendix — Excerpt from Business Plan

## Projected Financial Results for Liberty's Calgary Foothills Facility

|  | 2004 | 2005 | 2006 | 2007 | 2008 | 2009 | 2010 |
|---|---|---|---|---|---|---|---|
| Patient revenues | $1,000,000 | $1,500,000 | $1,800,000 | $2,000,000 | $2,500,000 | $3,000,000 | $3,500,000 |
| Care costs | $700,000 | $1,050,000 | $1,260,000 | $1,400,000 | $1,750,000 | $2,100,000 | $2,450,000 |
| Administrative costs | $500,000 | $500,000 | $500,000 | $500,000 | $500,000 | $500,000 | $500,000 |
| Marketing | $250,000 | $250,000 | $250,000 | $250,000 | $250,000 | $250,000 | $250,000 |
|  | $1,450,000 | $1,800,000 | $2,010,000 | $2,150,000 | $2,500,000 | $2,850,000 | $3,200,000 |
| Profit before taxes and depreciation | −$450,000 | −$300,000 | −$210,000 | −$150,000 | $0 | $150,000 | $300,000 |
| Number of patients | 10,000 | 15,000 | 18,000 | 20,000 | 25,000 | 30,000 | 35,000 |
| Capital expenditures (Diagnostic and care equipment) | $2,000,000 | $1,250,000 | $500,000 | $500,000 | $250,000 | $250,000 | $500,000 |

# ASHCOTT DENTAL OFFICE

## *Prem M. Lobo*

Ashcott Dental Office ("Ashcott") is a dental practice that was established in 1992 by four dentists who graduated from dental college together. The practice operates as a partnership, with net income calculated before tax at the partnership level and then allocated to the four partner dentists.

When Ashcott was created, the four partner dentists entered into a partnership agreement. The agreement stated that on a monthly basis, each dentist could receive partnership draws equal to 45% of their personal billings in that month. The remainder of the practice's billings, after deduction of operating expenses such as rent and hygienist salaries, was to be allocated to each of the four dentists on an equal basis.

In 2002, one of the partners, Dr. Fernandez, had a serious disagreement with the other three partners and indicated that she wished to withdraw from the partnership. She is no longer on speaking terms with the others and is no longer actively involved in management of the practice.

The partnership agreement states that in the event a partner wishes to withdraw from the partnership, the existing partners are obliged to purchase his/her share of the practice at fair market value. Dr. Fernandez has retained the firm of Rivard Taylor to determine the fair market value of her share of the practice based on the partnership's financial statements. The valuation and purchase of her share will occur in 2003.

The year 2002 was a particularly difficult one for the practice. Two competing practices had moved into the area and were aggressively soliciting patients. Expenses were higher than expected, and the practice had to replace most of its aging dental equipment.

It is now January 2003, and financial statements for the year ended December 31, 2002, are being prepared. In view of the difficulties experienced in 2002, the three active partners have voted to review some of Ashcott's accounting policies. They have hired you to conduct this review and to provide full and reasoned recommendations with respect to accounting treatments. You learn the following:

1. In 1992 the practice purchased a number of patient lists from the Ontario Dental Association. The lists were purchased for $100,000. Ashcott has been depreciating this in a straight-line manner over 20 years. In view of the increasing competition and the growth in the number of patients over the years, the partners wish to depreciate the remainder of the list in 2002.

2. Most of Ashcott's patients have dental insurance with large, established insurance companies. The insurance company is billed directly for the cost of services provided, and payment is usually received within 60 days. Ashcott accrues revenue when a patient receives treatment and a billing is issued.

3. On January 15, 2003, Ashcott learned that Imperial Insurance, which owed the practice $50,000 at December 31, 2002, had declared bankruptcy. It is extremely rare for a major insurer to go bankrupt.

4. The practice's existing dental equipment was aging and obsolete. Instead of purchasing replacement equipment using debt financing, the practice decided to lease its equipment through a financial leasing company. The leasing agreement Ashcott signed was for a term of 10 years, or virtually the full useful life of the replacement equipment, and provided for automatic transfer of ownership to Ashcott at the end of the 10-year term. On its balance sheet for December 31, 2002, Ashcott recorded a payable of $2,000, representing the monthly lease payment for December.

5. Ashcott maintains a limited inventory of dentures, adhesives, orthodontic accessories, and oral care products. In the past, inventory has been costed using FIFO. However, owing to the increased competition in 2002, most of the partners wish to use LIFO to "better reflect the cost of goods sold." The inventory value is $50,000 using FIFO, $25,000 using LIFO.

6. The dentists occasionally perform free procedures for those who have no dental insurance and who are unable to pay for necessary dental services. Performing occasional free procedures is seen as important in establishing goodwill in the community. In the past, "free" procedures have not been tracked by the accounting system. However, for 2002, the majority of the dentists wish to record the fair market value of such "free" procedures as a marketing expense.

7. During 2002, one of the partners, Dr. Zoff, hired his teenage daughter as Ashcott's office administrator. She was not paid for her services.

8. Early in 2002, Ashcott had to arrange for a line of credit with Norris Bank to help it cope with short-term cash flow needs. A restrictive covenant with Norris Bank specified that Ashcott had to maintain a current ratio of 1.5:1 at all times or repay its borrowings immediately. As at December 31, 2002, Ashcott had current assets of $765,000 and current liabilities of $480,000. Current liabilities included borrowings of $200,000 on the line of credit.

## Required

Prepare a report to the partners reviewing Ashcott's accounting policies. Provide well-reasoned recommendations with respect to the same. Be sure to discuss the impact of alternative accounting policies on the significant users of Ashcott's financial statements.

# XTREME PAINTBALL LIMITED

## *Dilsat Tuna*

Xtreme Paintball Limited (XPL), a private company, was incorporated in 1998. It is owned by three brothers — Sam, Tony, and Rocco. XPL manufactures and markets the paint capsules used in the sport of "Paintball." XPL also purchases paintball guns and sells them to its customers at a profit. XPL is the leading manufacturer of paintballs in Canada. In fact over 80% of all paintballs purchased in the Canada are supplied by XPL.

Over the years, North Americans have grown more and more interested in paintball. Many people, young and old, are now enjoying it. Paintball fans see the sport as both a hobby and an entertainment. Guns that resemble real guns are used to fire paintballs instead of bullets. The paintballs are manufactured in a specialized facility that encapsulates the paint in small balls. These capsules resemble "gelcaps" (cough and cold remedies are often come in similar capsules).

Because the paintball manufacturing process is so capital intensive, XPL has had to borrow funds from a large bank to finance its operations. XPL has been able to reduce its debt load over the years but still relies heavily on its creditors for continued support and growth. The bank has never asked for an audit before. Recently, however, XPL's owners met with the bank to make some routine changes to the banking agreement and were told they would have to provide audited statements for the year ended December 31, 2004. Specifically, the bank now requires XPL to provide audited financial statements 90 days after year end. The bank has also stipulated that XPL must maintain a debt-to-equity ratio of no more than 1:2.

Sommer & Partners LLP (S&P) have been XPL's accountants for many years. It is now November 2004, and you are the senior accountant at S&P who has been responsible for XPL's year end in the past. Sam, Tony, and Rocco have asked you to come in before year end to help their controller establish accounting policies that will be consistent with the bank's new requirements. You meet the brothers and the controller and note the following:

1. XPL has spent more than $425,000 to date researching and developing machines to manufacture pharmaceutical and consumer goods. XPL's managers have concluded that the pharmaceutical industry requires third parties with the machines and expertise to fill gelcaps. Essentially, pharmaceutical companies would own the drug patents but would contract out to companies such as XPL the task of filling the capsules with the drugs. It seems that XPL has spent $175,000 on research and an additional $250,000 on development. XPL has capitalized the full $425,000 as an asset on its balance sheet.

2. During the year, XPL sold paintball inventory with a cost of $85,000 and a fair value of $96,000 to Diesel Paintball Supplies in exchange for 3,000 Model XT500 paintball guns. The XT500s can be purchased from various suppliers XPL deals with. The purchase price can range from $25 to $38 per unit. XPL sold similar guns to its customers for $28 per unit last month. The controller has not recorded this transaction because he doesn't know how. "It's really just like nothing happened," he tells

you. "We gave them inventory and they gave us inventory. That's why I didn't record anything."

3. In September 2004, XPL shipped a truckload of paintballs to Paramount Paintball (PP), a new customer in the United States. To make the terms of the sale attractive and to encourage future purchases, XPL structured the deal so that PP would not have to pay for the paintballs until they were sold to customers. For this transaction, XPL has recorded a sale of $223,000 and reduced inventory by $188,000.

4. During the year, XPL introduced an extended warranty service on some of the higher-end paintball guns that were sold to Paintball Entertainment Centres (in much the same way, a bowling alley lets patrons use the house bowling balls and rent bowling shoes). Total sales of paintball guns under warranty were $675,000. XPL has never offered a warranty before. The controller states: "It's hard to estimate how many of the paintball guns will come back for service and how much it will cost to have them repaired, so I did not record a warranty provision".

5. Sales of $450,000 were made to another American company, Eagle Rock Paintball Arena (ERPA). Just as it had with PP, XPL sweetened the deal with ERPA by offering a "six-month money-back guarantee for the full $450,000." Most of the sales to ERPA were made in November. Thus the return period will not have expired by XPL's year end (December 31). XPL has recognized all $450,000 of revenue for the above transaction.

## Required

Provide a report outlining your recommendations on accounting policies to the owners.

# ENVIRONMENTAL CONSULTING INC.

## K. Bewley

Environmental Consulting Inc. (ECI) is a private corporation that assesses environmental contamination of land and manages cleanup projects. ECI's main customers are refining and manufacturing companies, retail gas station chains, and banks that have taken contaminated properties as security for loans. Of ECI's common shares, 40% are owned by its president; ECI's four senior managers own 15% each. The business was established in 1990 and has been growing steadily over the last 10 years. ECI employs 30 engineers and technicians, who earn salaries and also receive annual bonuses based on the profitability of the consulting projects they bring to ECI.

ECI's business operations consist of the following:

1. ECI contracts with customers to conduct environmental assessments. There are three kinds of assessment projects: Phase 1, Phase 2, and Phase 3. Projects can take from six weeks to several years to complete.
2. Phase 1 projects are routine soil and water tests, so the costs and engineering hours are very predictable. Phase 1 projects usually take about six weeks.
3. Phase 2 projects involve establishing a plan to clean up a contaminated site. Costs for this phase are fairly predictable because standard procedures are used to assess the various available cleanup techniques and to determine the optimal methods based on cost/benefit analysis. Phase 2 projects take 12 to 18 months to complete.
4. Phase 3 projects involve actual cleanup procedures. The costs of these projects are highly variable. ECI contracts out many of the activities to construction companies and waste disposal services.
5. The main costs for ECI are the hours the engineers spend on the projects and the costs of contracting out. Chemical analyses are contracted out to several different laboratories. Earth moving is contracted mainly to one construction company that happens to be owned by one of the senior managers/shareholders. Waste disposal services are contracted out to several different companies.
6. Customers pay a 50% deposit at the start of Phase 1, then progress payments thereafter as the project proceeds. These are set out in each contract, but ECI managers attempt to have 100% of the cost covered before the job is 80% completed. On routine Phase 1 and Phase 2 projects, ECI will accept a fixed contract price. On more uncertain Phase 3 projects, cost-plus pricing is usually arranged.
7. ECI uses a time-and-billing system to keep track of the hours engineers spend on each contract. On the basis of these hours, the costs of fixed-price contracts are assessed, as are the additional billings required for cost-plus contracts and the engineers' annual bonuses. Like many engineering firms, ECI uses a multiple of 2.5 times salary to calculate the hourly rate charged to customers for engineers' time. On this basis, the engineers' average charge-out rate is $100 per hour.
8. A few years ago, three of ECI's engineers developed a software program called PMP. This has turned out to be a very valuable technology for monitoring the environment of a company's properties and manufacturing assets. At first ECI used this software

internally, and realized significant savings in its own consulting assignments. During 2000 a government agency paid ECI $450,000 for its own copy of the PMP software and to have it made compatible with its own computer systems. ECI used this money to develop a user interface and operating system compatibility for the government agency. Having made these enhancements, ECI realized that the software could also be sold as a package to many other customers. Another PMP software package was sold late in 2000 for $700,000 to a metal refinery. According to the time-and-billing records, the engineers spent about 3,300 hours developing the original PMP software, 500 hours making it operational at the government agency, and 650 hours customizing it for delivery to the refinery. According to the PMP engineers, the government agency's software has been completely operational as of January 2001. The government agency will now pay an annual support fee of $100,000 to ECI for further upgrading, support, and maintenance.

9. ECI's president is interested in selling the PMP technology as a separate business from ECI, because he would like to retire and start a new business. The proceeds from the sale of PMP would be used to buy out the president's 40% interest in ECI. A multinational engineering consulting firm has made a serious bid of $8 million for the PMP technology, but it wants to review financial information and other operating information relating to the technology and the two prior sales before closing the deal (i.e., it wants to perform "due diligence" investigations before committing to buy).

10. ECI has had small bank overdrafts from time to time. However, it has financed its growth mainly with retained earnings or by issuing common shares to the president and senior managers for cash, so it has had no need for financial statements other than for tax purposes. The ECI bank loan has grown considerably since the PMP development started, because the software development engineers continued to receive salaries even when they were not generating any consulting fees. ECI's banker has required higher personal guarantees from the shareholders, and also is requesting GAAP financial statements for ECI's December 31, 2000, year end.

## Required

You have been hired to assist the president by advising on accounting policies for ECI's operations that will be acceptable to the bank and helpful in selling the PMP technology. In particular, the president is looking for suggestions on how to recognize consulting revenues, how to account for PMP development costs, and how to account for revenues relating to the sales of PMP to the government agency and refinery.

## Required (bonus)

Assume instead the role of an accounting advisor to the multinational firm that is considering buying PMP. What would be a critical piece of information to obtain from ECI regarding the PMP technology?

# DIAMONDBIRD INC.

## K. Bewley

Diamondbird Inc. was started up a year ago by it sole owner, your friend Joe Diamond. The company is a wholesaler of computer components. Its sales are mainly to small-town computer shops, with credit terms of 30 days. Diamondbird only allows sales returns if components are defective, in which case Diamondbird can return the components to the manufacturer for full credit. During its first year of operations, the costs of the products Diamondbird sells have fallen steadily.

At the end of its first year, the company's accountant informed Joe: "Following generally accepted accounting principles, your company's revenue for the year is $650,000 and your operating expenses are $90,000. Your gross profit could be $150,000 or $200,000 and your pre-tax income could be between $10,000 and $42,000, depending on your choice of accounting policies for inventory costing and bad debts. Also, I expect your company will run out of cash within the next four weeks, so you will either need to invest more of your own money or obtain an outside loan to keep operating. The lower pre-tax income figure will result in a lower tax liability, which will save you some cash in the short-term."

Joe is very confused by the accountant's remarks, and tells you: "I thought the accountant would be able to tell me what the company's correct profit number is for the year and not be asking *me* what to do! Also, no matter which net income number is 'correct,' I'm making a profit, so why am I running out of cash?!"

Joe has asked you to explain the company's financial position and results, analyze the situation, and recommend a course of action.

## Required

Provide the advice requested by Joe.

# THRIFTY AIRLINES

## *Prem M. Lobo*

Thrifty Airlines ("Thrifty") is a privately owned charter airline operating in Canada. Thrifty has been growing since its inception in 1950. Currently it operates "no frills" charter flights between major cities across Canada. Thrifty was founded by the late World War Two fighter ace Jack "Quicksilver" Smith. Its common shares are currently owned by Jack's children and other members of the Smith family.

Even though it has been growing, in recent years Thrifty has experienced financial difficulties owing to competition from Air Canada and other charter carriers such as WestJet, increased operating costs arising from skyrocketing fuel prices, and — recently — the effects of September 11 on the travel industry. Despite best efforts, the Smith family has been unable to turn Thrifty around.

So, effective January 2002, the Smith family has hired a skilled airline executive – Mr. High Flier — to take over Thrifty's operations. Mr. Flier is reputed to be one of the best managers in the industry. The Smiths are certain that Mr. Flier is vital to Thrifty's future, so they have offered him a generous salary, plus a bonus based on 10% of Thrifty's after-tax net income. The family has agreed to let him manage operations without interference and will receive operating results through annual financial statements.

Recently the federal government introduced a new program to help financially strapped airlines. This new program offers low-interest loans and fuel subsidies to airlines that demonstrate financial need. To assess financial need, airlines are required to submit their year end financial statements to the local program office for analysis. The Smiths have decided that Thrifty must apply under this program, as they cannot keep covering Thrifty's cash flow shortfalls much longer. They plan to formally apply in May 2003, once Thrifty's financial statements for the year ended December 31, 2002, have been finalized.

The other options available for the Smiths are (a) sell equity or (b) issue debentures to the general public. They do not want to take either course, as they wish to keep control over the family business.

It is now April 2003, and the financial statements for the 2002 fiscal year have to be finalized. Given recent events, the Smiths have decided to conduct a review of the company's accounting policies and have hired you to advise them on appropriate accounting policies. You learn the following:

1. Thrifty's flight employees are represented by two unions — the United Pilots Federation and the Union of Flight Attendants. The Smiths have tried but failed to renegotiate the unions' contracts to reduce salaries and benefits in order to conserve cash flows in these difficult times.
2. During 2002 the Smiths agreed to issue a class of special preferred shares to a wealthy Middle Eastern investor. The shares pay a dividend of 10% of face value, and the dividends are cumulative. The shares are retractable from 2007 onwards at the option of the investor for a price equal to their par value. Also, the shares are redeemable by the company at any time for a price equal to 1.5 times their par value. These special preferred shares do not have voting privileges.

3. During 2002, Thrifty made a strategic investment in Super Airways ("Super"), an American carrier. Thrifty and Super have partnered for extensive transit and transfer arrangements for their passengers. The investment of $15 million has given Thrifty a 21% voting ownership of Super. In 2002, dividends of $2.1 million were received from Super. As a gesture of good faith, Thrifty did not exercise its voting privileges and so is not represented on Super's board of directors. During 2002, Super reported net income of $100 million.

4. With Mr. Flier's efforts, Thrifty signed an agreement with the Toronto Maple Leafs ("the Leafs") to have their logo painted on the exterior of all its airplanes. The logo will remain on the aircraft for two years. As per the agreement, the Leafs paid Thrifty $5 million on signing and will pay $1 million each month for the duration of the agreement. The first year of the agreement is guaranteed, but after that either party can elect to discontinue it.

5. To increase sales, Thrifty has begun offering loyalty rewards, or "Thrifty Miles." Customers receive a certain number of these miles for each flight they travel on, which they can eventually use for free flights. Redemption of free flights is subject to blackout periods during March break and the Christmas season; otherwise, there are no restrictions. This program began only in 2002, so few customers have saved enough Thrifty Miles for free flights; thus it is not possible at present to estimate redemption rates. However, it is believed that customers will find the program attractive.

6. To conserve cash, Thrifty has obtained some spare parts for its aircraft from Slomas Aerospace. In return, Thrifty has agreed to provide the company with a considerable number of free flights for its employees at any time and on any route. The spare parts cost $2 million. The retail price of the free flights is estimated to be $1.5 million. The operating costs (fuel, salaries etc.) of providing the free flights are estimated to be $1 million.

7. To motivate employees to consider the best interests of the company, in 2002 Mr. Flier introduced a stock option plan. Based on work performance, employees receive a certain number of stock options during each fiscal year. The options can be exercised (i.e., used to purchase common shares of Thrifty) after three years, provided the employee is still working at Thrifty. Most employees remain with Thrifty for at least 10 years. An independent accountant hired by Thrifty has calculated that the fair market value of the stock options issued in 2002 was $2 million.

8. Also in 2002, Mr. Flier purchased some aircraft maintenance equipment from the recently bankrupt Canada 2000 for $250,000. The equipment was old and required significant repairs and maintenance, which cost $1 million. Mr. Flier feels that the equipment has been restored to a nearly new condition and will last for at least five years before being scrapped. New equipment of similar type and use would have cost nearly $3 million.

9. The Smiths do not want to prepare more than one set of financial statements.

## Required

Prepare a report to the Smith family that reviews and critiques Thrifty's accounting policies and provides recommendations.

# WORTH THE WAIT

## *Kevin Markle*

Robyn Hannah recently realized her lifelong dream by purchasing a flower farm. She has worked for the past 15 years as a nurse while studying horticulture part-time. The farm, called Worth The Wait Farm (WTW) has 100 acres of growing fields, three greenhouses, and two large barns. It had been in the family of the previous owners for more than 100 years, so there was no mortgage on the property when she bought it and the farm was not an incorporated entity. Before purchasing the farm, Robyn reviewed the previous three years' financial statements, which had been prepared for tax purposes only. Each of the years showed net income of between $100,000 and $120,000.

The farm cost $1,500,000. Robyn had $200,000 from her own savings and investments over the past 15 years, and she contributed all of it towards the cost of the farm. She was able to obtain a mortgage for $750,000 from a bank. The mortgage carries an interest rate of 6% and is secured by the farm's assets. The bank does not require an audit, but instead wants to receive an independent appraisal of the market value of the assets every two years. Robyn has also been able to obtain a line of credit from the bank to help finance daily operations. The maximum amount on the line of credit is $200,000; interest on any amount outstanding is 5%. Under no circumstances can she use the line of credit towards the purchase of the farm or for large capital purchases.

The remaining $550,000 has been financed as debt with the farm's seller. The details of this debt are given below. Besides the interest and principal to be paid as described below, the sellers are entitled to receive 15% of all reported net income in excess of $25,000 for each quarter that the debt remains outstanding.

Robyn has come to you for help with some accounting and business decisions she must make. She does not have any training or background in accounting. She is quite concerned that the farm (and her with it) could go bankrupt because it is so highly leveraged as she starts out. There is a bookkeeper at the farm whom she will continue to employ. He has been working for the farm for 23 years and so is very comfortable with how things are accounted for. Robyn would like you to review the information she has given you and write a report to her that recommends any changes that should be made or that explains why the current treatment is still acceptable. Robyn also wants the report to tell her whether she can quit her job as a nurse (at which she makes $50,000 per year) and work full-time on the farm. The sellers have told her she can ask them any questions that come up, so she asks you to identify any issues for which you need more information.

You have obtained the following information:

1. The sale of the farm closed on January 1, 2004. The farm has always had a December 31 year end, and Robyn wishes to keep this, since the income from the farm will be going on her personal tax return.

2. The terms of the debt to the seller are as follows: Robyn will pay the seller $38,500 (7% of the principal) in interest each December 31, with the first payment to be made in 2004. The $550,000 in principal is to be paid in full on December 31, 2014.

3. 85% of the farm's revenue comes from sales to large wholesalers that supply flower shops all over Ontario. The wholesalers provide WTW with a schedule of their anticipated demand for the entire year in November of the preceding year. WTW then purchases seeds and sets its growing schedule according to the demand. Revenue from the sales to the wholesalers has always been recognized when the flowers are shipped to them.

4. Over the past three years, WTW has started leasing its farm equipment instead of purchasing it. WTW always takes long-term leases on the equipment and intends to buy the equipment for a bargain price when the leases start to expire. The only things related to the leases on the financial statements are the lease payments made each year.

5. The previous owner of the farm experimented a fair bit with crossing types of flowers and developing higher-quality plants. All costs related to these experiments were recorded as the asset "Product development" and amortized over seven years. Robyn does not intend to pursue any such development for the foreseeable future.

6. The following is the income statement of WTW:

### Worth The Wait Farms
### Income statement for the years ended December 31

|  | 2003 | 2002 |
|---|---|---|
| Revenue | 1,200,000 | 1,080,000 |
| Cost of goods sold | 500,000 | 450,000 |
| Gross margin | 700,000 | 630,000 |
|  |  |  |
| Wages expense | 225,000 | 220,000 |
| Amortization of equipment | 55,000 | 75,000 |
| Amortization of development | 60,000 | 45,000 |
| Lease expense | 120,000 | 100,000 |
| Loss on sale of equipment | 40,000 | — |
| Other expenses | 100,000 | 80,000 |
|  |  |  |
| Total expenses | 600,000 | 520,000 |
|  |  |  |
| Net income | 100,000 | 110,000 |

## Required

Prepare the report to Robyn Hannah.

# XENON INC.

## *V. Umashanker Trivedi*

Xenon Inc. was incorporated five years ago on January 1. The following events relating to Xenon took place during the course of the current year (2001):

1. On January 1, 2001, Xenon Inc. issued to the public two thousand $1,000 10% five-year serial bonds, ⅕th maturing every year for the next five years, at 90% of their face value. Interest is payable annually on the first day of the following year.

2. The proceeds from the bond issue were used to construct a building to house Xenon's corporate headquarters. The building was completed on June 30, 2001, and is estimated to have a useful life of 30 years. Xenon proposes to depreciate the building using the CCA methods allowed for tax purposes. It believes that this is a "rational" method of amortization. The bonds payable have been secured against the new building.

3. Equipment purchased five years ago for $40,000 was sold for $35,000. Amortization expense for all equipment for the year was $100,000. However, the "Accumulated amortization" account increased by only $80,000 for the year. The book value of this equipment for tax purposes is $15,000.

4. To replace the above equipment, Xenon has leased new equipment for three years. The estimated useful life of the equipment is five years. The market value of the equipment is $500,000. The monthly lease payment is $7,000. Xenon has the option of buying the equipment at its fair market value at the end of the lease term.

5. On January 15, 2002, one of Xenon's past customers paid the entire amount of the $150,000 it owed Xenon. Xenon had written off this amount two years earlier as uncollectible.

6. During the year, Mr. Argon, Xenon's CEO, died suddenly. Xenon had a life insurance policy on Mr. Argon for $5 million. The proceeds have not been received as of year end. Related monthly premiums paid are $2,000.

7. Revenues from sales during the year were $1.5 million. Expenses, including those detailed above, came to $1.2 million. The statutory tax rate effective for Xenon's current year is 40%, and for all future years is 50%. Furthermore, Xenon expects to be profitable in the foreseeable future. It is now January 31, 2002.

The new CEO, Mr. Radon, has approached you to determine the correct way of accounting for the above events.

## Required

Prepare a report to Mr. Radon describing the accounting implications of the above events and indicating how he should account for the same in his accounting book. Make and state clearly necessary assumptions where required.

# WORLDCAN

## *Kevin Markle*

WorldCan Inc. is a large Canadian company that has been in business for more than 15 years. It has been a leader in the growing telecommunications sector for the past 10 years. The shares of WorldCan are traded on the Toronto Stock Exchange. The share price enjoyed a five-year streak of consistent growth. However, it has recently plummeted, in the wake of news that WorldCan's CEO has been charged with fraud. Furthermore, the company's CFO has resigned and may face similar charges. The accusations and charges all have to do with the accounting decisions that had guided the preparation of the annual financial statements over the previous six years.

WorldCan's directors are shocked by the recent turn of events and are trying to do what they can to save the company. To that end, they have hired a new management team, including a new CFO. The board's primary goal is to get the company's accounting policies straightened out so that it can present "clean" financial statements to its shareholders as soon as possible. To ensure that the decisions are made with objectivity, the board has hired you to advise the CFO on the policies that should be used. The board wants you to write a report to the CFO detailing your recommendations. Wherever possible, the directors want the report to include the numerical impact of your recommendations. The report will be reviewed by the board and may be made available to the regulators as proof of the improvements that are being made.

You have visited the offices of WorldCan to review its accounting records and spoken to the authorities investigating the former CEO and CFO, and have uncovered the following information:

1. The accusations against the CEO and CFO centre on the fact that they allegedly "shifted" a number of large liabilities off the company's balance sheet. This came to light when WorldCan defaulted on an interest payment to a bank from which the company had borrowed a very significant amount of money.

2. WorldCan began leasing all its manufacturing equipment two years ago and records the annual payments as lease expenses. Because the machines tend to become unreliable after 10 years, they typically lease them for just 7 years. Per the agreement that WorldCan has with the lessor, WorldCan never purchases the equipment at the end of the lease term. Under the agreement, it was able to lease the following equipment in 2002 and 2003:

| Date of lease commencement | Cost of equipment if purchased | Annual lease payments | Lease term | Implied interest rate |
|---|---|---|---|---|
| Jan 1, 2002 | $10,000,000 | $1,700,000 | 2002 – 2008 | 5% |
| Jan 1, 2003 | $15,000,000 | $2,300,000 | 2003 – 2009 | 4% |

3. WorldCan has a defined contribution pension plan. There is nothing related to this pension plan on the balance sheet of the company.

4. WorldCan provides three-year service contracts to its customers. The customer is required to pay for the entire three years up front, and the payment is nonrefundable. The contract entitles the customer to no-charge service on its equipment for the life of the contract. WorldCan has always recorded all contract payments as revenue on receipt of cash.

5. When the stock price began to rise in 2000, WorldCan began offering many of its key employees stock options as a form of compensation. This had two very positive effects: it helped increase employee loyalty, and it allowed the company to retain more of its cash. Nothing related to the stock options has ever been reported in the financial statements.

6. WorldCan has a December 31 year end. The scandal broke in November 2003.

## Required

Draft your report to the new CFO.

# WILLOWS INC.

## K. Bewley

Willows Inc. is a private corporation that owns and operates a golf course on a lakeside property in southern Ontario. The company was founded 20 years ago by Alice Green and now is operated by her son, Brian, who owns 100% of the common shares. Since it started up, the business has operated an 18-hole golf course as well as a clubhouse with a restaurant and pro shop. Willows's main revenues are greens fees (what customers pay for playing a round of golf), food and beverage sales, and pro shop sales of golf equipment and clothing.

About two years ago, Brian and three other local businesspeople decided to develop townhouses on land owned by Willows that is adjacent to the golf course. A separate corporation, Lakeside Lifestyle Homes Limited (LLH), was established to develop the townhouse units. Willows put the land into LLH in exchange for 25% of the common shares. The other three investors each have 25% of the LLH common shares, for which they paid cash ($400,000 each). Brian manages the LLH operations; the other shareholders are not actively involved.

A marketing study done for LLH indicates that over the next 20 years there will be a demand for retirement homes with a "lifetime lease" arrangement. Based on this study, LLH will lease the townhouses to residents on a "life lease." Each resident will pay a fixed monthly amount for the rest of his or her life. LLH will retain ownership of the townhouses, the land, the roads, and all the common areas. A resident will be able to cancel the lease at any time by giving LLH three months' notice. Residents will be entitled to unlimited use of the Willows golf course.

The LLH shareholders decided to develop the property in phases. Phase 1, 30 townhouse units, was developed using the funds provided by the LLH shareholders and a construction loan from a local bank. Further development will depend on the success of Phase 1. If further development is done, the LLH shareholders plan to finance it by issuing long-term debt to a pension fund. There is enough land to build an additional 100 units. Phase 1 of the development is now almost complete, and the shareholders are pleased with its success. Sixteen units have been leased, and many interested potential residents have visited the property since it opened for inspection two months ago.

Brian has hired you as an accounting advisor to LLH and has provided you with the following information:

1. Thirty identical townhouse units have been built in Phase 1, plus roads, electricity, and water services for the community. Costs incurred during the two years of development are shown in the table at the top of the next page.

| Construction materials and labour for townhouses | $3,000,000 |
|---|---|
| Construction costs for roads, water, and electricity | 80,000 |
| Interest on construction loan | 200,000 |
| Brian's salary for managing Willows and LLH | 140,000 |
| Advertising, promotion, and legal fees related to leasing the townhouses | 30,000 |
| Cost of market research study | 66,000 |
| Dividends paid by LLH ($11,000 each to Brian and the other three shareholders) | 44,000 |

2. All that is left to be done to complete Phase 1 is the landscaping, which will cost an estimated $25,000. Brian would like to know how these costs should be accounted for in the current and future years. The townhouses are expected to last for at least 30 years.

3. In addition to their fixed "life lease" payments, townhouse residents will pay an annual maintenance fee to LLH at the beginning of each year of the lease, to cover costs of maintaining the properties and common areas. The lease agreement allows for these maintenance payments to be increased if justified by increases in LLH's operating costs. The lease agreement requires LLH to provide audited annual financial reports to residents on the maintenance and operating costs of the property. Brian wants to know how the annual fees should be accounted for and what information should be collected for the annual report to the residents.

4. Brian has had discussions with the pension fund representatives regarding obtaining long-term debt financing for LLH through a private placement. The pension fund manager has indicated that prior to approval of the debt issue, LLH would be required to provide audited general-purpose financial statements for its most recent year end and other information the pension fund might request. For long-term debt to be granted to LLH, the pension fund would require audited financial statements annually. The pension fund would take the LLH townhouse property as collateral and would require LLH to meet debt covenants based on its debt-to-equity and working capital ratios.

5. One of the shareholders is considering selling her investment in LLH in the near future and has asked Brian to prepare a report of what she can expect to receive for her common shares.

## Required

Brian has asked for your advice on how to report these matters in the financial reports LLH would be required to provide the pension fund. He also wants an overview of any income tax implications for LLH. Provide the requested advice.

# BACCHUS INC.

## V. Umashanker Trivedi

Mr. Apollo and Mr. Zeus incorporated a new company, Bacchus Inc., on January 16, 2001, by contributing capital of $1 million: $300,000 in cash and the rest in inventory of Greek wine of fine vintage. The inventory of wine cost Mr. Apollo and Mr. Zeus $250,000 at time of purchase, but is now estimated to have a fair market value of $700,000. Mr. Apollo is actively involved in running the business and is its CEO; Mr. Zeus is simply half-owner of the company. The following events took place during the year:

1. Mr. Apollo issued to the public 2,000 five-year bonds at $1,000, each bearing an interest rate of 10%, at 90% of their face value on July 16, 2001.
2. The proceeds from the bond issue were used to build a combination headquarters and winery. The building was still under construction at year end. The building, once complete, will have an estimated useful life of 30 years. Bacchus proposes to depreciate the building over its useful life using the straight-line method, assuming a salvage value of $25,000. Under tax rules, buildings are depreciated using the declining-balance method, assuming a useful life of 20 years.
3. Bacchus decided to lease all its winemaking equipment for a term of four years, making monthly lease payments of $30,000. The expected useful life of the equipment is six years. The winemaking equipment, if bought today, would cost $1.45 million. Bacchus has the option to buy the winemaking equipment at estimated fair market value of $300,000 at the end of the lease term of four years.
4. Bacchus sold wines that it valued at $75,000 for $150,000 during the year. However, Bacchus had received only $100,000 of the purchase price by year end and expects $40,000 to be received next year. The balance of $10,000 is expected to go bad next year.
5. Revenues during the year (including the $150,000 above) were $1.5 million. Expenses, including those detailed above (but not those stated below), came to $1 million.
6. Bacchus was fined $50,000 by the local municipality for inappropriate disposal of grape waste. In addition, one Mr. Tipsy is claiming that he inadvertently stepped on the grape waste and slipped and fell as a consequence, breaking his hip. Mr. Tipsy has filed a lawsuit against Bacchus. Bacchus' lawyers believe there is a high probability that Bacchus will lose the case and face damages of $100,000 when it is finally decided two years from now. Mr. Apollo thinks Bacchus should wait until the case is decided before accounting for the loss.
7. The statutory tax rate effective for Bacchus' current year is 40% and for all future years is 30%. Bacchus expects to be profitable in the foreseeable future.

Mr. Apollo has approached you to determine the correct way to account for the above events.

## Required

Prepare a report to Mr. Apollo indicating how he should account for the above events in his accounting book. Make necessary assumptions where required.

# HADDOCK FISHERIES

## *Prem M. Lobo*

Haddock Fisheries Inc. ("Haddock") is engaged in fishing operations in Newfoundland. The shares of Haddock are owned by Jack Cod, who started the company in 1966.

Haddock's workforce is unionized. The current employment agreement is set to expire on April 30, 2002. Talks between management and the union have been unsuccessful so far. The union reps note that the company has been profitable in the past and are negotiating for a three-year contract with a 10% annual wage increase each year plus an upfront signing bonus of $5,000 for each of Haddock's 100 employees. Management has refused any increase, declaring that "we just don't have the cash to pay you any more than we presently do."

Union officials have been provided with excerpts from the audited financial statements at Haddock's year end of February 28, 2002 (see below). The financial statements were prepared in accordance with GAAP. Union officials have also compiled a list of information obtained during discussions with management.

**Haddock Fisheries Inc.**
**Balance Sheet as of 28 February 2002, in '000s**

| | | |
|---|---:|---:|
| ASSETS | | |
| Cash | | 750 |
| Accounts receivable, net of allowance | | 5,750 |
| Inventory | | 740 |
| Marketable securities | | 1,250 |
| Future income taxes | | 1,000 |
| | | 9,490 |
| | | |
| Property, plant, & equipment | | |
| Fishing vessels | 20,600 | |
| Plant and equipment | 4,850 | |
| Fishing licences | 1,500 | 26,950 |
| Investment in Maritime Fisheries Corporation | | 3,000 |
| Investment in lobster storage technology | | 5,000 |
| | | 34,950 |
| | | |
| TOTAL ASSETS | | 44,440 |
| | | |
| LIABILITIES AND OWNERS' EQUITY | | |
| Accounts payable | 3,510 | |
| Loan payable, current portion | 3,300 | 6,810 |
| Loan payable, long-term portion | | 28,150 |
| | | |
| Total liabilities | | 34,960 |

Equity

| | | |
|---|---|---|
| Common shares | 2,000 | |
| Retained earnings | 7,480 | 9,480 |
| TOTAL LIABILITIES & OWNER'S EQUITY | | 44,440 |

## Haddock Fisheries Inc.
### Income Statement for Year Ended February 28, 2002     In '000s

| | | |
|---|---|---|
| Revenue – fishing business | 30,000 | |
| Cost of sales – fishing business | (21,000) | |
| Gross margin | | 9,000 |
| | | |
| Wages | (3,000) | |
| Interest | (2,100) | |
| Amortization | (1,600) | |
| Bad debts | (1,000) | |
| Amortization of investment in lobster storage technology | (300) | |
| General and admin | (370) | |
| Gain on asset swap | 800 | (7,570) |
| Operating income (loss) | | 1,430 |
| | | |
| Equity in earnings, Maritime Fisheries Corporation | 1,000 | |
| Loss on writedown of securities | (500) | 500 |
| Income before income taxes | 1,930 | |
| Income taxes – current | (650) | |
| Income taxes – future | 71 | (579) |
| Net Income | | 1,351 |

## Notes from discussions with management:

1. Revenue is recognized on fish sales when product is packaged and shipped to customers. Haddock guarantees the freshness of its product and offers refunds and discounts in the event that customers are dissatisfied with its products in any way. Also, most customers are given extended payment terms as an incentive to purchase from Haddock. Typical payment terms are 60 days.

2. Haddock accounts for marketable securities at the lower of cost and market. Haddock's auditors wrote down marketable securities by $500,000 at year end owing to ongoing declines in the stock market, which affected the market price of its securities. Management invested in the securities in order to redeploy excess cash that was on hand. The original intent was to hold the securities for a short period and then sell them in time to purchase inventory during the lobster season (see point 3 below).

3. Haddock invested a considerable amount to develop its lobster storage technology. It expensed money spent on laboratory research and feasibility assessment of the technology. However, the technology has since proved to be a success, and Haddock has capitalized all further expenses related to prototype construction, testing, and laboratory work. Haddock decided to amortize its investment in the lobster storage technology straight-line over 20 years based on the expected useful life of the technology to Haddock. Annual cost savings from utilizing this technology are estimated as $300,000 in 2002; those savings may increase in subsequent years.

4. In 2001, Haddock invested $2,500,000 in Maritime Fisheries Corporation ("Maritime"), a rapidly growing fisheries company based in Halifax. This gave Haddock a 20% ownership in Maritime. Haddock is accounting for this investment using the equity method. Haddock has no representation on Maritime's board of directors but is a major supplier of live lobsters to Maritime. The investment was made in order to diversify Haddock's business risk.

5. At year end 2002, Haddock reported equity in earnings of Maritime of $1,000,000 and a net investment in Maritime of $3,000,000.

6. Haddock depends on bank loans to finance its investment in fixed assets, particularly its fishing vessels and factory facilities. Owing to the relatively large amounts of money advanced to Haddock, the bank has demanded audited financial statements to be provided to it within 30 days after each year end. In addition, the bank requires Haddock to maintain a current ratio of 1.2:1 at all times during the year or risk having its loans called in immediately.

7. In 2002, Haddock engaged in an asset swap with Grand Bank Trawlers Inc. ("Grand Bank"). Haddock exchanged 100,000 pounds of frozen scallop inventory for one of Grand Bank's fishing licences. The exchange was correctly recorded at the fair market value of the inventory exchanged, and Haddock recognized a gain of $800,000 on the sale.

8. Haddock has a fleet of two fishing vessels. Government regulations state that each vessel must be dry-docked and completely refitted and overhauled once every four years. The following information pertains to past refit expenses:

|  | Last refit | Cost of last refit |
|---|---|---|
| Vessel 1 | May-98 | $500,000 |
| Vessel 2 | Feb-99 | $600,000 |

Haddock has chosen not to accrue an amount for these refit expenses as the actual amount that needs to be spent can be accurately determined only once each vessel is in dry dock.

9. Future tax assets arose because Haddock's amortization policy for fixed assets was faster than the respective CCA amortization rates for tax purposes.

10. Haddock was named as defendant in a lawsuit involving the collision of one of its fishing vessels with a luxury yacht. The owners of the yacht have alleged negligence on the part of the vessel's captain and have sued Haddock for $2,000,000. Haddock's

legal counsel has stated that Haddock has a strong defence and that the likelihood of losing the lawsuit is remote. Per GAAP, Haddock did not record any amount on its financial statements.

## Required

Union officials have hired you to analyze the financial information provided. Specifically, the union wants you to analyze Haddock's cash flow prospects in both the short and long term and to assess the company's ability to meet its salary and bonus demands. Be sure to state what additional information you want to have in order to complete your cash flow analysis. Give your reasons.

# CHAPTER 8

# ADVANCED CASES

This chapter provides a set of "advanced" cases. They are classified as advanced because they require an extended analysis, deal with more complex materials, or simply require you to process more information before making your recommendations. Regardless of the complexity of the case, however, the analysis process remains the same. If you use the process that has been illustrated in this book you will find that even advanced cases are now within your abilities.

The final case in the chapter reflects "a day in the life of an ethical financial controller." This case is unique in that it provides you with a timetable of events in one day of a controller's work and personal life. This case is a reminder that business decisions do not come prepackaged with just the right information to provide a technical solution. In fact, in some cases the most difficult part of a decision will be recognizing that you *are* making a decision and that there *are* alternative ways to handle matters. This case is also a reminder that business decision making has an ethical dimension. The decisions you make in your career will have consequences both for you and for the many stakeholders who rely on your decisions.

# C. WEBB

## K. Bewley

Mr. and Mrs. Webb hope to provide cash to their son Cobb, who has just qualified as a registered pharmacist, so that he can start up a pharmacy business. After paying for his education, Cobb has only $1 to invest in the business. The Webbs' other son, who is a lawyer, advises his parents that they should not just give cash to Cobb directly. He recommends that they take either debt, in the form of a note payable by the pharmacy corporation, or preferred shares of the corporation. The Webbs cannot take common shares because by law only a registered pharmacist can own the common shares of a pharmacy corporation. The pharmacy will start small, but it is expected that it will grow substantially over the next five years because it is located in an area where many new homes and businesses are being built. The Webbs are planning to retire in a few years, and the cash they would be providing to Cobb's business is a large part of the money they have saved for their retirement.

## Required

Discuss the implications of these ways of providing financing for the pharmacy business from the perspective of both the Webbs and the pharmacy corporation. Which would you recommend, and why?

# RC PLAYERS LTD.

## *Kevin Markle*

Karen Rives and Joel Collins are old friends who met in university in 1990, when they were in a play together. After graduating, they went their separate ways and built successful careers, Karen as a fundraising professional, Joel as a lawyer. In the summer of 2003 they got reacquainted and started talking about old times. Each now learned that the other had been thinking about leaving current employment and launching a theatre company. They agreed at that time that they would keep their current jobs; but they would also start laying the groundwork (developing a business plan and strategy) for a theatre company in their spare time.

On June 7, 2004, RC Players Ltd. (RCP) was incorporated, with Karen and Joel each purchasing 50 shares in the company at $1 per share. Many theatre companies are run as not-for-profit organizations; Karen and Joel want to run their company as a for-profit business so that all future profits will belong to them as shareholders. They are certain that if they succeed, a large theatre company will want to buy their company from them.

RCP ran its first play, *Oleanna,* in September and October 2004. The show ran for six weeks and was well received by critics and the public. Over 75% of the available seats were sold — a success by theatre standards. The production covered its costs, and RC was able to retain more than $20,000 in cash once all bills had been paid.

The second show was a musical, *Batboy.* It was scheduled to run for six weeks in December 2004 and January 2005 but closed early (after three weeks) because reviews were harsh and ticket sales were poor. This left RCP with no cash and a significant amount outstanding on its line of credit with a local bank.

It is now April 12, 2005. Karen and Joel have come to you, an accounting expert, for help with RCP's financial statements. They have not bothered with financial statements so far, but the bank has recently called them to ask about the amount outstanding on the line of credit, so they now realize they need statements. Ever since *Batboy's* failure, they have been worried the company will fold. They want you to recommend appropriate accounting policies for RCP. They have chosen a May 31 year end for the company.

You have collected and reviewed information on the company's transactions and have had many discussions with Karen and Joel, and have found the following:

1. The business plan calls for RCP to put on four shows each year, one of them a musical. The shows will run for six weeks starting March 1, June 1, September 1, and December 1 of each year. Each show will be preceded by a four-week rehearsal period. The plan calls for only two shows in the 2004–05 year (*Oleanna* and *Batboy*), so there will not be another show this fiscal year.

2. To produce *Oleanna*, RCP needed $250,000 of cash. Karen and Joel approached several banks, but none would lend money to RCP, considering it too risky. One bank

agreed to extend a line of credit to RCP and set a floating maximum for the line of credit so that RCP could have $1 outstanding on the line of credit for each $1 of shareholders' equity that was reported on the balance sheet.

3. Karen inherited $150,000 in the summer of 2004 from a distant aunt and decided she would put $90,000 of it into the company. To keep the control of the company equal between her and Joel, the company issued nonvoting preferred shares to Karen in exchange for the $90,000. The preferred shares have a cumulative annual dividend equal to 3% of the reported net income and are retractable. Joel did not have any savings, so he could not put any cash in. However, they agreed that he would do all the legal work for the company and would receive compensation for his work in the form of preferred shares (of the same class as Karen's) until he held the same value of shares as her. After that, he would be paid in cash or they would hire a different lawyer.

4. The remaining necessary funds were obtained in the form of sponsorships from corporations. RCP sold three levels of sponsorships:

   - *Act I* — sponsor pays $10,000. For this it can place a small ad in the program of one show, have its logo placed on the poster for the show, and receive four complimentary tickets to one show.
   - *Act II* — sponsor pays $25,000. For this it can place a large ad in the program of two shows, have its logo placed on the poster for each show, and receive six complimentary tickets to two shows.
   - *Finale* — sponsor pays $50,000. For this it gets everything the Act II sponsor gets, but for four shows. It will also be the "title sponsor" for two of the shows (meaning all posters and announcements will say "Presented by XYZ Corporation").

   RCP sold four Act I's and two Act II's prior to *Oleanna* opening and three more Act I's prior to *Batboy* opening. Just last week, they reached an agreement with a major corporation for a Finale sponsorship for the upcoming season. They will receive the $50,000 in mid-April. They have also sold five Act I's for *Forever Plaid* (see point 6) and five Act II's for the upcoming season.

5. One of the Act II sponsors filed a lawsuit against RCP in February 2005 after *Batboy* failed. They are asking for their $25,000 back, plus an additional $40,000 in damages that resulted from their association with the show. Joel is handling the case and intends to fight it in court. A trial is scheduled for November 2005.

6. The next show, a musical called *Forever Plaid,* will open on June 1, 2005. There is good buzz about the show in the city, and as of today the show is already 80% sold out through advance ticket sales totalling $576,000. Interest in the show was generated through an extensive ad campaign that was launched in March. The campaign cost $180,000. RCP also expects to spend $300,000 by the end of May for the building of sets and the payment of actors and directors for the rehearsal period.

7. RCP has signed a five-year lease on a 500-seat theatre in Toronto. The lease gives the company exclusive use of the theatre and can be renewed at RCP's option for up to 25 years. The monthly rent for the theatre is $8,000. If RCP wants to get out of the lease before the end of the first five-year term, it will have to pay 40% of the total amount still outstanding (i.e., 40% × number of months to end of lease × $8,000) at the time of termination of the lease.

## Required

Prepare the report for Karen Rives and Joel Collins.

# BOTTLEFAB CASE

### Catherine Byers

Your client, Bottlefab Corp. ("Bottlefab"), manufactures and sells plastic bottles for packaging. Sales are generated through contracts for thousands of units to food companies (such as Kraft) and health and beauty aid manufacturers (such as Procter & Gamble). Senior managers participate in a bonus plan that is based on growth in pre-tax income over the prior year, sourced from the company's audited financial statements.

You are the audit manager and are preparing for the audit for the year ended December 31, 2003. Today is February 15, 2004, and you have just concluded a meeting with your client's new controller, who has provided the following information regarding Bottlefab's activities. This controller is an accomplished accountant in her homeland, but she is new to this country and wants to make sure she adheres to Canadian accounting standards.

1. When a sales contract is for a specified quantity of bottles, two years may elapse prior to its completion. A shipment consists of 1,000 bottles on a pallet, and the customer can request delivery of anywhere from 1 to 100 pallets at a time. Sales are recorded when the individual shipments are delivered to the customer as contracts are filled. Terms are 2% — 10 days, net 30 days. Most customers take the discount, and the controller records the net sale when the shipment is made.

2. On June 30, 2003, the company leased five new PCs for its offices. The lease terms specify six semiannual equal payments of $1,985.03, with the first payment due and paid December 31, 2003. The controller recorded the payment as an expense in the income statement. The interest rate implied in the lease was 6%, the fair market value of the equipment was $10,000 when it was acquired, and Bottlefab can buy all of the computers for $1 at the end of the lease.

3. In July 2003, Bottlefab's director of operations utilized excess capacity by accepting and fulfilling an emergency order from a new customer for revenue of $300,000. Bottlefab's president did not like the deal but accepted it anyway. Shortly after Bottlefab shipped the order, the customer called to say the bottles did not match specifications and that its corrosive product was seeping out of them, causing damage at its distributors' premises. Bottlefab's new customer filed a lawsuit for $1 million against the company. Bottlefab's quality-assurance team ran a battery of tests and found that the bottles matched and in some cases exceeded the customer's specifications. Bottlefab's counsel advised that the lawsuit is not likely to succeed; however, the president is concerned about protecting the company's good reputation and wants to settle out of court for $400,000.

4. On November 1, 2003, Bottlefab took delivery of and title to a new piece of manufacturing equipment and agreed to pay the supplier $100,000 in equal instalments of $50,000 on the first and second anniversary of delivery. The market rate of interest is 5%. The director of operations estimates that it took the shop steward three man-weeks to install the machinery and get it up and running. The shop steward earns $100,000 per year. The controller is unsure what amounts to capitalize for the new machinery.

5. On November 15, 2003, Bottlefab sold a piece of manufacturing equipment for $45,000. The purchaser agreed to pay in full by February 15, 2004. Bottlefab booked the portion of the annual amortization expense just prior to the sale. At the time of sale, the machine's cost was $60,000 and accumulated amortization was $20,000. The controller credited the full amount of the proceeds to the asset account.

6. The bottles are made from plastic pellets purchased from a recycler. Pellet costs have been rising, and the director of purchasing arranged in mid-December 2003 to buy 1,000,000 pounds for $0.50 per pound. The FOB point is the supplier's loading dock, and Bottlefab must pay for transportation costs to its factory. The director of operations estimates that this supply contract will last for 15 months of production. The contract starts January 1, 2004.

7. The first shipment under the supply contract was destroyed in January 2004, when the transport truck jackknifed, struck a bridge abutment, and burst into a fireball. To maintain production lines, the director of operations purchased an emergency supply of 70,000 pounds of pellets for $70,000. The controller wants to record an increase to cost of sales in the December 31, 2003, financial statements equal to the cost of the replacement inventory purchased as well as $100,000 for any loss from lawsuits brought by the truck driver or bridge owner.

## Required

Assume the role of audit manager in charge of the Bottlefab audit. Draft a letter to the controller outlining your firm's position with respect to any financial accounting and financial statement presentation issues you have identified.

# SIMPLE DIAGNOSTIC MEDICINE

## *A. Scilipoti*

The famous Dr. Jack Pillule incorporated Simple Diagnostic Medicine (SDM) in 1985. SDM manufactures a special urine-testing device of Dr. Pillule's design. Over the years, SDM has grown its test division and now performs numerous medical testing procedures for Canadian hospitals and medical practitioners. Pillule's motto is "Keep It Simple." SDM has focused its attention on high-margin, high-turnover testing procedures, and these have generated stable earnings and operating cash flows.

In recent years, SDM has started two new divisions. In 1997 it began a separate division through its 70% owned Simple Research Company (SRC). SRC performs R&D testing for SDM and other drug companies as well. In 1998 the company decided to build (using a federal government subsidy) a new production facility for nuclear medical testing components. Dr. Pillule is excited about the prospects for the new divisions. The testing facility has grown rapidly and over the past year has completed three additional corporate acquisitions.

SDM is growing so rapidly that it requires additional financing. The company is already listed on the Toronto Stock Exchange but has approached The Drug Group (DG) with a 25% investment opportunity. SDM's shares have been trading recently at $10, and the company has 100 million shares outstanding. The acquisition price has been set at 10 times SDM's 2000 net income. DG is a large investment firm that typically makes equity investments in drug-related organizations.

Dr. Pillule is quite proud of SDM's accomplishments. At a recent shareholders' meeting he explained that in spite of the company's recent investments and new divisions, it continues to generate consistent growth in corporate earnings and cash from operations. He points out that even the company's liquidity ratio has improved over the prior year. Dr. Pillule is excited that the market for outsourced R&D is expected to grow by 20% in the coming year and that the market potential for nuclear testing devices is "explosive."

Attached (pages 185 to 187) are the company's financial statements and notes for the past two years ended December 31, 2000 and 1999. Also attached are additional items provided by SDM's controller.

## Required

You have been hired by DG to evaluate the SDM investment opportunity and recommend a course of action. DG will require a thorough analysis of the company's overall financial statement presentation and the inclusion of all information that you feel will be relevant to its decision. Your recommendation must be supported. Do not limit your analysis to a list of ratios without interpretation.

### SIMPLE DIAGNOSTIC MEDICINE
### CONSOLIDATED BALANCE SHEET
### PERIOD ENDED DECEMBER 31, 2000 & 1999
### 000'S OF CANADIAN DOLLARS

|  | 2000 | 1999 |
|---|---|---|
| **ASSETS** | | |
| **Current Assets** | | |
| Cash | 13,200 | 47,500 |
| Accounts receivable (Note 1) | 63,600 | 43,800 |
| Other receivables (Note 2) | 8,700 | 3,200 |
| Inventory (Note 3) | 40,400 | 25,700 |
| Prepaids | 3,200 | 4,900 |
| **Total Current Assets** | 129,100 | 125,100 |
| | | |
| Investments (Note 4) | 28,000 | 21,200 |
| Deferred development costs (Note 5) | 12,600 | 2,500 |
| Capital assets (Note 6) | 34,000 | 11,200 |
| Intangible assets (Note 7) | 125,700 | 97,800 |
| Other assets | 0 | 3,800 |
| **TOTAL ASSETS** | 329,400 | 261,600 |
| | | |
| **LIABILITIES & SHAREHOLDERS' EQUITY** | | |
| **Current Liabilities** | | |
| Accounts payable | 38,600 | 22,400 |
| Accrued liabilities | 17,200 | 11,700 |
| Current portion of debt (Note 8) | 24,300 | 69,600 |
| Deferred taxes | 7,800 | 4,000 |
| **Total Current Liabilities** | 87,900 | 107,700 |
| Long-term debt (Note 8) | 154,000 | 101,600 |
| | | |
| **TOTAL LIABILITIES** | 241,900 | 209,300 |
| | | |
| **SHAREHOLDERS' EQUITY** | | |
| Common stock | 23,100 | 22,900 |
| Retained earnings | 64,400 | 29,400 |
| **TOTAL SHAREHOLDERS' EQUITY** | 87,500 | 52,300 |
| | | |
| **TOTAL LIABILITIES & SHAREHOLDERS' EQUITY** | 329,400 | 261,600 |

## SIMPLE DIAGNOSTIC MEDICINE
## CONSOLIDATED STATEMENT OF CASH FLOWS
### PERIOD ENDED DECEMBER 31, 2000 & 1999
### 000's OF CANADIAN DOLLARS

|  | 2000 | 1999 |
|---|---|---|
| **OPERATING CASH FLOWS** | | |
| Net income | 35,000 | 20,000 |
| Charges not affecting cash | | |
| Amortization | 23,000 | 29,800 |
| Amortization of intangible assets | 15,400 | 9,800 |
| Deferred taxes | 3,800 | 2,100 |
| Changes in non-cash working capital | | |
| Changes in accounts receivables | (19,800) | (10,000) |
| Changes in inventory | (14,700) | (10,600) |
| Changes in other receivables | (5,500) | (1,000) |
| Prepaids | 1,700 | 1,500 |
| Accounts payable | 16,200 | 5,000 |
| Accrued liabilities | 5,500 | 1,000 |
| **NET OPERATING CASH FLOWS** | 60,600 | 47,600 |
| | | |
| **INVESTING CASH FLOWS** | | |
| Corporate investments | (50,100) | (20,500) |
| Deferred development costs | (10,100) | (2,500) |
| Capital investments | (42,000) | (29,200) |
| Other assets | 3,800 | 100 |
| **NET INVESTING CASH FLOWS** | (102,200) | (52,200) |
| | | |
| **FINANCING ACTIVITIES** | | |
| Long-term debt | 7,100 | 7,000 |
| Common shares issued | 200 | 100 |
| **NET FINANCING ACTIVITIES** | 7,300 | 7,100 |
| | | |
| **INCREASE (DECREASE) IN CASH** | (34,300) | 2,500 |
| **OPENING CASH BALANCE** | 47,500 | 45,000 |
| **CLOSING CASH BALANCE** | 13,200 | 47,500 |

**SIMPLE DIAGNOSTIC MEDICINE**
**CONSOLIDATED INCOME STATEMENT**
**PERIOD ENDED DECEMBER 31, 2000 & 1999**
**000's OF CANADIAN DOLLARS**

|  | 2000 | 1999 |
|---|---|---|
| **REVENUE** | | |
| Medical testing procedures | 570,000 | 560,000 |
| Outsourced research | 380,000 | 140,000 |
| **TOTAL REVENUE** | 950,000 | 700,000 |
| | | |
| **COST OF SALES** | | |
| Medical testing procedures | 480,000 | 420,000 |
| Outsourced research | 198,000 | 86,000 |
| **TOTAL COST OF SALES** | 678,000 | 506,000 |
| | | |
| **GROSS PROFIT** | 272,000 | 194,000 |
| | | |
| **EXPENSES** | | |
| Selling general and administrative costs | 120,000 | 88,000 |
| Interest | 54,000 | 26,300 |
| Research costs (Note 5) | 11,000 | 9,500 |
| Amortization on capital assets (Note 6) | 23,000 | 29,800 |
| Amortization of intangible assets (Note 7) | 15,400 | 9,800 |
| **TOTAL EXPENSES** | 223,400 | 163,400 |
| | | |
| **INCOME BEFORE TAXES** | 48,600 | 30,600 |
| | | |
| Current taxes | 9,800 | 8,500 |
| Deferred taxes | 3,800 | 2,100 |
| | | |
| **NET INCOME** | 35,000 | 20,000 |

## Notes to the Financial Statements, 2000 and 1999

1. Accounts receivable: The company records a 1% allowance for all accounts receivable balances over 120 days old.
2. Other receivables: The balance includes receivables from Dr. Pillule dating from 1991. The amounts are due on demand and do not bear interest. To date no amounts have been repaid.

3. Inventory: Inventory cost is determined using absorption costing. In 2000 the inventory balance included $8,000,000 or 100% of the total advertising costs associated with new nuclear testing procedures.
4. Investments: The company makes investments in certain research and development joint ventures. Investments are accounted for using the CICA guidelines according to the company's investment interest.
5. Deferred development costs: Development costs are deferred if they meet the CICA criteria. All other research costs are expensed as incurred.
6. Capital assets: Buildings are depreciated over 50 years, cars are depreciated over 10 years, and computer equipment is depreciated over 5 years, on a straight-line basis. $22,800,000 relates to the "building under construction" included in the company's balance sheet. No amortization has been recorded for the building under construction.
7. Intangible assets: Intangible assets are amortized on a straight-line basis over 30 years. The majority of the balance came from the recent 2000 acquisition of TLQ. TLQ has a patent for the manufacture of AZT, the highly successful AIDS drug, which expires in 2010.
8. Long-term debt: The debt bears interest at 10.5% and is due in 2005. The repayment schedule over the next five years is as follows:

| 2001 | $24,300 |
| 2002 | $95,000 |
| 2003 | $20,000 |
| 2004 | $20,000 |
| 2005 | $19,000 |

The long-term debt holders require a total debt-to-equity covenant of at least 2:1.
9. Revenue recognition: Revenue for SRC is recognized when the research project is signed regardless of cash collection. Revenue from testing procedures is recognized when it meets the CICA requirements.

## Notes Received From the SDM Controller

1. Dr. Pillule explains that the doctors sometimes take a long time to pay but they always pay.
2. Receivables from startup medical research firms represent 45% of the 2000 balance and 25% of the 1999 balance.
3. In 2000, the company changed the expected useful life for buildings from 25 years to 50 years.
4. Included in the buildings under construction is $12,000,000 of interest costs.
5. Investments include a 19.5% interest in Test It. Test It recorded a loss of $55 million in 2000.
6. SDM's VP-Finance is paid a 5% bonus based on the company's net income.
7. The term of a standard medical drug patent in Canada is between 16 and 20 years.

# A DAY IN THE LIFE OF AN ETHICAL FINANCIAL CONTROLLER

*Elizabeth LaRegina*

The life of a financial controller or chief accountant can be hectic and varied. In a typical organization, the controller is responsible for the completeness and accuracy of financial information, for making accounting policy decisions, for watching corporate expenses and expense accounts, and for dealing with auditors. To survive, the financial controller must contend with pressures from many directions, including management, staff, and head office.

In the course of a day, a financial controller may need to make a number of decisions, many of which have ethical implications. These decisions can be very difficult, and the controller may need to weigh his or her own values, career prospects, and organizational loyalty. The following chronicles the day of a "not so typical" financial controller who is faced with many ethical challenges.[1] It is your task to identify the ethical decisions this controller has made or needs to make, and to provide your opinion as to whether that person did the right thing.

## Welcome to My World . . .

8:30 a.m.: Well, my day at work begins and as usual I've started by reading *The Globe and Mail*. It's very important to read it from cover to cover every day — that's what they told us in business school! It's the best way to keep up to date. I see that one of our competitors has been caught in a $30,000 insider trading mess. (Checked out the movie section to see what is coming out this week.)

9:00: Opened up my day timer to check on meetings. Good, not many meetings today, but lots of e-mails. You can just tell year end is coming up from the number of e-mails people are sending.

9:15: My assistant drops off a five-inch-thick pile of "rush" invoices and expense reports for my signature. She says she is going downstairs for coffee, do I want one? Absolutely, I say.

9:20: The CEO comes into my office, sits down, and talks about golf for 20 minutes. On his way out, he mentions that since this year our company's net income is going to be pretty weak due to the economy, let's make sure we book everything — expenses, any writeoffs — *anything* we possibly can. I agree with him, it only makes sense. If we are not going to get bonuses this year, why not book everything now, so that we have a clean slate for next year? The investment analysts and shareholders are already expecting results that are down from last year.

9:45: Assistant comes in with cold coffee — didn't want to interrupt the business meeting. Oh well.

10:00: Executive support calls. The trading window during which executives are allowed to make transactions in our shares ends today. Can I confirm that I want to sell

[1] Issues raised in this case study are largely drawn from recent newspaper items. The case is not based on any particular organization or specific individual(s).

1,000 shares today? Our new house is closing next week, everyone at home is really excited about this. I need the cash soon for the lawyers, so I say yes. I checked the stock price and it sure looks good right now. I'm really glad I got in there before the trading window closed, or I wouldn't have been allowed to sell my shares.

Signed one inch of invoices in one minute. Hmm. Gotta get my speed up.

11:00: Telephone budget meeting with regional managers. I gave them their final approved expense budgets for next year. I told them that their budget for next year was based on their 9 months' actual expenses, annualized for 12 months. You should have heard the squawking. Not fair, what about our year end costs? What year end costs, I say? This isn't the way we did it last year! So what, I say.

Noon: Lunch with Bob, one of our best salespeople. His sales are phenomenal this year and he's making a ton of commission. I'm glad he suggested Canoe, one of my favourite restaurants. I offered to pick up the tab but he grabbed the bill first, so I guess it will go through his expense report, not mine. Too bad he's breaking up with his wife Sherrie. During lunch he asked me if we could delay his year end commission payments to some time later next year. He's trying to keep his income as low as possible so that it won't be included in his divorce settlement. I'll make a note to do it. None of my business really, but we always like to accommodate top salespeople where we can.

1:35 p.m.: Back to the grind. More invoices. Maybe I shouldn't have had the calamari at lunch!

Drafted the "Accrual Policy for Managers." At this time of the year, we always send out a note to remind all the managers to process any expenses they may have and set up accruals for any expenses they have incurred but not yet paid. I used last year's policy note but I put some extra emphasis on the importance of expense accruals this year. I think the CEO will like that, given our earlier conversation about booking everything we possibly can.

2:00: Went downstairs for a coffee and ran into another of our top salespeople. He says to me in the lineup that he's been told he's going to be audited by the government tax department. No big deal, but just so I know, on the form T2200 the company filled out for him for inclusion with his tax return, he "whited out" some of the information we put in. In particular, he "ticked" the box saying he was required under the terms of his employment to supply his own assistant. With the box now "ticked," he could do some income splitting with his wife.

"Whoa," I said. "That's the company form telling the government tax office about the nature of your employment. You know we don't make you pay for your own assistant. Hey, what you deduct is between you and the government, but just don't go messing with our forms and changing the information the company provides." I told him that if the tax department calls, I'll be telling them the truth, that's it, that's all.

2:30: Met with our external auditors regarding year end procedures. I had a nice discussion with the new audit manager. He doesn't seem to know much about our business but is very pleasant. He presented me with a schedule and list of documents for year end.

3:00: Sent a note to my assistant, Sandy, to make sure to go back through this year's invoices, entries, and anything else the auditors usually look at, to check for my signature. I might have missed something earlier in the year. Best to be sure that everything looks good.

3:30: Wow, this has been a tough day. I can just feel the year end tension approaching. The CEO stops by again and doesn't talk about golf, thank goodness. He has decided to hold a big conference for the whole company in March, two months after year end. (Yee-haw, sounds like fun!) He has just been talking to the Professional Party Planning People (PPPP), and they can bill us right now so we can get the cost in this year's expenses. We can work on the details of the conference later; they'll even let us change our minds about it if we want to. No obligation. I drafted the accrual entry and sent it in for processing. I hope I get more stock options this year, for this kind of wizardry.

4:00: Bob the financial analyst comes in to talk about a family problem overseas. His mother is very ill. (He's the guy who has done year end audit schedules for the past five years.) Hmmmn ... this could be trouble. Cindy, the other person who is cross-trained on the desk, is eight months pregnant. Better start getting someone else going in there. Heaven forbid that I have to do the year end schedules myself! I'm sure I don't know how!

4:30: Looked at e-mails. Wow, more than 50 since this morning. One is from Compliance saying that insider trading is a problem and that they will be doing a company review. I guess they saw the same article this morning I did.

5:00: I better get going soon. Hockey tickets tonight. It was really nice of those consultants to get them for me. My nine-year-old is really excited about this. He's never been to a live game before.

6:15: Spaghetti and salad for dinner with my favorite garlic bread. Treated myself, had two helpings. A simple dinner is great after such a fancy lunch.

7:30: Made it in time for the first faceoff. Hey, the CFO is here too! I see him down in the 100 section. Guess I didn't rate! I need to make a mental note to scrutinize those consultant invoices extra closely tomorrow.

9:50: Wholly mackinaw, our team won 3-2! Time to fight the crowds and go home.

## The next day . . .

8:30 a.m.: Phone call from some new company Human Resources Ethics person. I have to go to their offices right away. I wonder what they want to talk about?

## Requirements

1. In the course of the day, this financial controller has made several ethical decisions. Identify the ethical issues that arise in the case. Why do you believe these are ethical issues? What criteria can you use to define what constitutes an ethical issue?
2. For each of the issues raised, provide your opinion as to what the controller did or should have done.
3. Should a financial controller be attuned to ethical issues more than or less than or the same as other members of senior management? Explain.

# C H A P T E R 9

# WHAT SHOULD YOU DO NEXT?

This book has provided you with an opportunity to develop your case analysis skills by applying them to a set of realistic business transactions. This required you to exercise your judgment and critical thinking skills in identifying issues, creatively generating alternative approaches to these issues, evaluating the consequences of implementing your alternatives, and recommending a course of action. These are the skills that mark successful managers, consultants, accountants, and auditors. So what must you do next in order to further refine your skills? You need three things: substantive knowledge, institutional knowledge, and rhetorical skills.

## SUBSTANTIVE KNOWLEDGE

Case analysis requires you to identify issues and generate alternatives. Both these skills are enhanced if you have theoretical frameworks to work with. Imagine how life appears to a new-born baby before it has the ability to focus clearly and before it has concepts to help it organize the images and sounds it experiences. William James suggested that without some preconceptions we would see life "as one great blooming, buzzing confusion."[1] Similarly, Friedrich Nietzsche rejected the dogma of "immaculate perception"[2] — the very idea that we can perceive the world without using the concepts that already exist in our mind. Case analysis thus depends on the richness of the theoretical frameworks or models to which you have been exposed. How else can you understand what you are seeing?

Economic and social life is complex, and many disciplines have tried to help us make sense of it. At a minimum you should have some exposure to the models of economics, sociology, and psychology. Economic models provide a guide to the world assuming rational and individualistic behaviour — that is, everyone is out for their own gain regardless of others. Sociology tries to understand how people's behaviours

---

[1] *The Principles of Psychology*, Cambridge, MA: Harvard University Press, 1981 [1890], p. 462.

[2] Online at http://www.luminary.us/nz/zarathustra.html. Accessed July 29, 2005.

are conditioned by the social groups to which they belong, including families, religions, political parties, organizations, and nations. Psychology looks how individuals process information and react to their external environment and how individual differences affect those processes. All three disciplines provide partial but important insights into business behaviour. Use your elective courses to broaden the variety of perspectives to which you are exposed.

The models of these disciplines are used in the business literature with specific application to the problems faced by markets, organizations, and individual decision makers. You will see applications of these models in business courses in organizational behaviour, marketing, finance, and accounting. A difficult but important skill for you to acquire is using the models and frameworks you are exposed to in these courses to analyze real business problems. As your knowledge of these models and frameworks grows, you will find it easier to identify issues and alternatives in any setting you analyze.

## INSTITUTIONAL KNOWLEDGE

Institutions are the rules, norms, and procedures we use to organize our lives. Some institutions, such as laws and the rules governing stock markets, are formal and codified; others are informal and tacit — for example, the norm of reciprocity in gift giving, and how ambiguities in the law are treated on a day-to-day basis in a given society at a particular point in time. Institutions are both constraints on what we can do and resources for us to draw upon in order to get things done. In case analysis, an understanding of the institutions that affect actors and their decisions is absolutely crucial to making good recommendations that can be implemented.

Formal institutional knowledge is taught in many business courses such as law, financial accounting, and tax. In these fields, institutions have been codified over many years and are enforced by the state and the courts. It is essential for you to understand these institutions. Informal institutional knowledge is more difficult to teach but is embedded in all business courses as part of the background — a background that is often taken for granted by both the instructor and many students. Informal institutions include the social norms that have developed to help people coordinate their actions. They may be arbitrary, but people expect others to behave according to them. People who violate these norms make other people uncomfortable and less willing to engage in relations with them.

One professor wanted his students to understand the effect of violating social norms, so he had students do things out of the ordinary and observe the reactions they got. Try these experiments at your own risk! One student stood at a restaurant window and simply watched people eating.[3] Another went into a nearby store and tried to bargain for the price of a toothbrush. In business, social norms affect the

---

[3] I thank Professor Pat Bradshaw for this example.

clothes we wear, the way we address others, and the verbal agreements we make and keep. This type of knowledge can only be gained through observation and experience.

Students from other countries often find informal institutions the most difficult and perplexing part of their education. When you have not been exposed to a particular set of informal norms all your life, it is difficult to understand why people behave in a certain way when there is no obvious reason for it. Courses in international business provide useful exposure in this regard; students can acquire a better understanding of informal norms by seeing their own country through the eyes of others. International exchanges can also make students more sensitive to these issues.

Note that there is nothing wrong with identifying alternatives that violate institutional norms, be they formal or informal. Before making a recommendation, however, you must evaluate these norms to determine how binding they are and how costly it would be to change a norm. For example, it was once illegal to open a retail store on Sunday, but many firms decided that it was worthwhile opening anyway and paying a fine each time. Meanwhile, they lobbied to have the law changed to reflect changing informal norms.

Many informal norms are captured in the term "ethics." It is important to recognize that business decisions have far-reaching consequences and that everyone involved in those decisions must consider whether both the process and outcomes of these decisions are ethical. Ethics cannot be reduced to a simple set of rules. Like case analysis, ethical decision making is based on a set of principles applied with diligence to complex circumstances. There are legitimate debates about what is ethical in a given circumstance and what standards should be applied. The most important thing is that ethical considerations be part of the decision process.

## RHETORICAL KNOWLEDGE

Rhetoric is the use of language to persuade. Many parents tell their children "use your words" as an alternative to using violence to resolve disagreements. Society is based on the exchange of words in various forms. We use written and verbal contracts in business, provide verbal or written instructions to others, and attempt through words and images to convince our customers to buy our products and services. Classic Greek teaching saw rhetoric as a cornerstone of democracy.

Case analysis requires you to use words to convey the process you went through in reaching your conclusions. Even more importantly, it requires you to offer a convincing rationale for your recommendations. In classic rhetoric there are three bases on which you can support your argument: logic, emotion, and character. An appeal to logic posits that the recommendation is the most efficient way to achieve a given objective; an appeal to emotion, that the recommendation meets some set of values important to the decision maker; an appeal to character, that the recommendation is supported by those whom the decision maker would like to emulate.

In most situations the recommendations you make should be supported by logic, but this may not always be possible. Also, given the decision maker's objectives, a logical solution (narrowly defining logic to mean the most efficient way to achieve a given outcome) may not be the best or most feasible in the circumstances. Also, in a given case there may be multiple alternatives that are equally logical but you must still provide a single recommendation. In these latter situations a deadlock between two alternatives may be resolved by appealing to emotional or character-based grounds.

Rhetoric is an art. It is taught in some business communications courses, but in most schools it is taught by having you write memos, letters, and reports and make presentations. In arts and humanities courses, rhetoric is treated more explicitly, and you may benefit from a course in this area.

## CONCLUSION

This book has perhaps provided your first exposure to a case-based approach to learning and to a principles-based approach to financial reporting. This approach is increasingly being seen as an effective way to teach students the skills they require in order to succeed in business and professional life and as a necessary approach to financial reporting.

We hope you have enjoyed working through these cases, arguing with others about what should be done, and defending your approach to issues. Remember that case analysis is less about the end point than about the journey. The point of this book has been to help you develop a set of skills that will last a lifetime.

### ITHACA[4]

When you start on your journey to Ithaca,
then pray that the road is long,
full of adventure, full of knowledge.
Do not fear the Lestrygonians[5]
and the Cyclopes and the angry Poseidon.
You will never meet such as these on your path,
if your thoughts remain lofty, if a fine emotion
touches your body and your spirit.
You will never meet the Lestrygonians,
the Cyclopes and the fierce Poseidon,
if you do not carry them within your soul,
if your soul does not raise them up before you.

---

[4] I thank John B. Dowling for first bringing this poem and its message to my attention and I thank M.S. Hershcovis for reminding me to apply it in my life.

[5] Lestrygonians, Cyclopes, and Poseidon are all "monsters" in Greek mythology. The poet is telling us to not be afraid of these or other imaginary gremlins.

Then pray that the road is long.
That the summer mornings are many,
that you will enter ports seen for the first time
with such pleasure, with such joy!
Stop at Phoenician markets,
and purchase fine merchandise,
mother-of-pearl and corals, amber and ebony,
and pleasurable perfumes of all kinds,
buy as many pleasurable perfumes as you can;
visit hosts of Egyptian cities,
to learn and learn from those who have knowledge.

Always keep Ithaca fixed in your mind.
to arrive there is your ultimate goal.
But do not hurry the voyage at all.
It is better to let it last for long years;
and even to anchor at the isle when you are old,
rich with all that you have gained on the way,
not expecting that Ithaca will offer you riches.

Ithaca has given you the beautiful voyage.
Without her you would never have taken the road.
But she has nothing more to give you.

And if you find her poor, Ithaca has not defrauded you.
With the great wisdom you have gained, with so much experience,
you must surely have understood by then what Ithaca means.

— CONSTANTINE CAVAFY[6] (1868–1933)

---

[6] *The Complete Poems of Cavafy* by C.P. Cavafy. Trans. Rae Dalven. New York: Harcourt, 1976.

# CREDITS

**Page 3**

Figure 1.1: From Benjamin S. Bloom et al., *Taxonomy of Educational Objectives, Book 1: Cognitive Domain.* Published by Allyn and Bacon, Boston, MA. Copyright © 1956, 1984 by Pearson Education.

**Page 11**

Transat non-GAAP measures: From www.transat.com/en/media_centre/2.0.centre .asp?id=876. Reprinted with permission.

**Page 14**

Figure 2.1: Reuters (Vancouver), March 11, 2000. Reprinted with permission.

**Page 22**

Figure 2.2: Reprinted with permission from KPMG LLP, the U.S. member firm of KPMG International.

**Page 26**

Figure 3.1: From C.C. Lundberg and C. Enz, 1992, "A Framework for Student Case Preparation," *Case Research Journal* 13 (summer); 144. Reprinted with permission from the North American Case Research Association.

**Pages 196–197**

"Ithaca" from *The Complete Poems of Cavafy*, copyright © 1961 and renewed 1989 by Rae Dalven, reprinted by permission of Harcourt, Inc.